# How to Establish a
# UNIQUE BRAND
## in the
# CONSULTING
# PROFESSION

*Powerful Techniques
for the Successful Practitioner*

## ALAN WEISS, Ph.D.

**JOSSEY-BASS/PFEIFFER**
A Wiley Company
www.pfeiffer.com

*The* ULTIMATE
CONSULTANT
*Series*

Published by

# JOSSEY-BASS/PFEIFFER
A Wiley Company
989 Market Street
San Francisco, CA 94103-1741
415.433.1740; Fax 415.433.0499
800.274.4434; Fax 800.569.0443

www.pfeiffer.com

Jossey-Bass/Pfeiffer is a registered trademark of Jossey-Bass Inc., A Wiley Company.

ISBN: 0-7879-5513-2

**Library of Congress Cataloging-in-Publication Data**
Weiss, Alan
How to establish a unique brand in the consulting profession: powerful techniques for the successful
practitioner / Alan Weiss.
p. cm.—(The ultimate consultant series)
Includes index.
ISBN 0-7879-5513-2 (alk. paper)
1. Business consultants. 2. Consultants—Marketing. I. Title.
II. Series.
HD69.C6 .W4595 2002
001'.068'8—dc21
2001002023

Printed in the United States of America

We at Jossey-Bass strive to use the most environmentally sensitive paper stocks available to us. Our
publications are printed on acid-free recycled stock whenever possible, and our paper always meets
or exceeds minimum GPO and EPA requirements.

Acquiring Editor: Matthew Holt
Director of Development: Kathleen Dolan Davies
Development Editor: Leslie Stephen
Editor: Rebecca Taff
Senior Production Editor: Dawn Kilgore
Manufacturing Supervisor: Becky Carreño
Interior Design: Gene Crofts
Illustrations: Lotus Arts

Printing 10  9  8  7  6  5  4  3  2  1

*This is dedicated to*
*Trotsky,*
*the world's greatest dog*

# Also by ALAN WEISS

*Books*

*The Ultimate Consultant* (2001)
*Getting Started in Consulting* (2000)
*The Unofficial Guide to Power Managing* (2000)
*How to Market, Brand, and Sell Professional Services* (2000)
*Good Enough Isn't Enough* (1999)
*How to Write a Proposal That's Accepted Every Time* (1999, 2002)
*Money Talks* (1998)
*Million Dollar Consulting* (1992, revised edition 1998)
*Our Emperors Have No Clothes* (1995)
*Best Laid Plans* (1991)
*Managing for Peak Performance* (1990)
*The Innovation Formula* (with Mike Robert, 1988)

*Booklets*

How to Maximize Fees
Raising the Bar
Leadership Every Day
Doing Well by Doing Right
Rejoicing in Diversity

*Audiocassettes*

*Peak Performance*
*The Consultant's Treasury*
*The Odd Couple*®

*Videos*

*Stories I Could Never Tell: Alan Weiss Live and Uncensored*
*Alan Weiss on Marketing*
*Alan Weiss on Product Development*

*Newsletters*

*Balancing Act: Blending Life, Work, and Relationships* (electronic)
*The Consultant's Craft*
*What's Working in Consulting* (editor)

# *About the Author*

**A**lan Weiss began his own consulting firm, Summit Consulting Group, Inc., out of his home in 1985 after being fired by a boss with whom he shared a mutual antipathy. Today, he still works out of his home, having traveled to fifty-one countries, forty-nine states, published sixteen books and over four hundred articles, and consulted with some of the great organizations in the world, developing a seven-figure practice in the process.

His clients have included Merck, Hewlett-Packard, State Street Corp., Fleet Bank, Coldwell Banker, Merrill Lynch, American Press Institute, Chase, Mercedes-Benz, GE, American Institute of Architects, Arthur Andersen, and over two hundred similar organizations. He delivers fifty keynote speeches a year and is one of the stars of the lecture circuit. He appears frequently in the media to discuss issues pertaining to productivity and performance and has been featured in teleconferences, video conferences, and Internet conferences.

His Ph.D. is in organizational psychology, and he has served as a visiting faculty member at Case Western Reserve, St. John's, and half a dozen other major universities. He currently holds an appointment as adjunct professor at the graduate school of business at the University of Rhode Island, where he teaches a highly popular course on advanced consulting skills. His books have been translated into German, Italian, and Chinese.

*The New York Post* has called him "one of the most highly regarded independent consultants in the country," and *Success Magazine,* in an editorial devoted to his work, cited him as "a worldwide expert in executive education."

Dr. Weiss resides with his wife of thirty-two years, Maria, in East Greenwich, RI.

# Contents

N o one in his right mind places investments with the obnoxious caller at 8:30 in the evening who barges into his home life to announce that there awaits him rare titanium futures for a mere $40,000 investment sent to a post office box in Hoboken, New Jersey. No one in her right mind would buy consulting services in that manner, either, yet that's how most consultants insist on selling them.

Look at almost any consulting firm's promotional literature or website, and you'll find one of two approaches. There will be unrelenting claims of tremendous competence and capabilities, and exhaustive descriptions of methodologies, approaches, technologies, and models. Or the approach will be so "soft" and generic—and otherwise vague—as to produce confusion as to whether this is a consulting operation or a storm door company. In either case, what's in it for the potential client is largely conspicuous by its absence.

But this book isn't for those consultants. It is for the successful professionals who understand that acquiring business is about convincing the prospect that a partnership will improve the latter's condition by a huge multiple of whatever investment is required. I would hope that the reader has already completed the keystone book in this series, *The Ultimate Consultant*. But, in any case, whether you are a large firm partner, a small firm owner, or a solo practitioner, you should be someone constantly searching for a better way to attract customers to you, to develop a word of mouth about your expertise, and to create the "gravity" that draws others to your firm.

No one cruises the highways to read billboards, and no one seeks out consultants in order to read their promotional materials or glorified self-praise. George Odiorne wrote once that "the successful man is one who has objective interests which absorb him, thus making him an object of interest to others." This book is for men and women who want others to seek them out because they have created a great interest in who they are and what they do.

Alan Weiss, Ph.D.
*East Greenwich, RI*
*July 2001*

# *Acknowledgments*

At the age of 54, I've led a full and rich life, perhaps the envy of most. I've learned that such great good fortune is only partially due to talent—and is largely due to family, friends, and happenstance.

My deepest appreciation for a loving, smart, strong-willed family, who had the confidence and strength to put up with me and ensure that my head never exceeded the size of our doorways: my wife and lover, Maria; daughter and television producer, Danielle; and son and actor, Jason.

Consultants always must thank the clients, from whom we learn so much. A special mention here to Roseann Stichnoth, at the Federal Reserve Bank of New York, and Keith Darcy of IBJ Whitehall for their trust and for what I've learned from them.

For the hundreds of people who have participated in my mentoring program over the years, keeping me in touch with the trials and opportunities of the profession at so many differing levels, my thanks for your trust and infusion of ideas and experiences.

My thanks to Phoebe for her energy and stimulation. And as always, through a never-imagined sixteen books, my thanks and profound admiration to L.T. Weiss, who knows more about life than any of us will ever be able to understand.

# A Brand by Any Other Name

*Why Consultants Desperately Need Brands to Thrive (Survival Isn't Enough)*

L et's cut to the chase. A brand is a recognition factor. It creates awareness in people's minds that you (or your firm) represent a particular quality in a certain area. It is a marketing force worth billions of dollars.

There was a time when people would say, "We are the Cadillac of the business." Cadillac had such a strong brand image as *the* height of luxury, quality, and success that "We are the Cadillac of the travel business" or "We are the Cadillac of the lawn care business" was neither an uncommon nor a bizarre statement. (I once saw a wholesale catalog for funeral directors cite the most expensive product as the "Cadillac of coffins," which also offered some nice alliteration.)

Yet Caddy's brand statement has pretty much been lost. People say today, "We are the Mercedes of the business." Just as

1

no one would claim "We're the Taurus of the business," citing yourself as the Cadillac today might well prompt a customer to say, "Well, that's nice, but I want the Mercedes of the business, thank you very much."[1]

Cadillac lost its brand "gold standard" through poor quality, a plethora of other General Motors cars at much lower prices that resembled it too much, and competitive inroads that brought Cadillac back to the rest of the pack. All that time Mercedes was building a repute for quality, reliability, engineering "like no other car in the world," and high prices. Make no mistake, people believe they get what they pay for. Branding is more about the perception of excellent than about the perception of a good deal.

The value of the brand is that people purchase for the brand's own sake, and not with their usual amount of analysis, cynicism, or caution. When Mary Kay Cosmetics awards their top sales people, they buy them pink Cadillacs. No one asks what cars they would prefer or debates about buying a less expensive BMW. The Cadillac is their symbol of successful sales. Similarly, when people have finally "made it" in life, or received a promotion, or won a lottery, their first move would be to buy a Cadillac. They didn't compare gas mileage, compare financing, or ask about troublesome repair histories. They simply bought the brand that was equated with success.

It's no accident that *Fortune* magazine frequently shows a very powerful executive about whom it is doing a feature article posed in front of a Ferrari. Even though the individual is making $9 million a year, even though the stock price has shot through the roof, and even though *Fortune* has validated the success through the allocation of ten pages in the magazine, that one picture, with such a powerful brand of wealth and power, is added for credibility.

> Effective branding can create such a strong compulsion for the buyer to buy that routine caution, due diligence, and even vacillation are removed from the equation. That acceleration at the buying point is worth a lot of investment in the creation of the brand image.

[1]It's interesting that "We're the Rolls-Royce of the business" never really caught on. Branding is fickle. I think that Rolls presented too much of a snooty, eccentric image, while Mercedes is all about German engineering, comfort, and style.

I've talked about automobiles to this point because they are the most expensive single life style purchase that most people make.[2] Their "brands" have been so important to success that they are referred to rather regally as "marques."

## MARQUE MY WORDS: PERCEPTION IS REALITY

Brands create an attraction to a particular source of products or services, and that attraction is often so strong that normal discrimination, skepticism, and price sensitivity are subordinated. In the consulting business, that has meant that whenever an executive has had a strategy problem he or she has often said, "Let's see if McKinsey is willing to handle this." Just as no purchasing manager ever was fired for buying IBM hardware decades ago (because there was no higher quality to acquire, in everyone's perception, so if something went wrong it couldn't be blamed on the purchase decision), no one on the board could blame the CEO for a poorly constructed strategy if McKinsey has been helping out.

Perception is reality. There might well have been better hardware providers than IBM and there probably are firms that formulate strategy better than McKinsey. That's not important, because there is no empirical quality catalog that buyers consult.[3] The only thing that matters is what the perception of the buyer is, and it is the influencing of that perception which creates powerful brands.

Brands are fickle because perception is fickle. Boeing seemed to be the only name to consider in air frames, but a combination of its blunders and Airbus's initiatives has changed that significantly. We've watched foods such as meat, eggs, and fish whirl around as healthy, unhealthy, and healthy (again) choices.

An important aspect of branding is that it has as strong *negative* values as positive values. In my mentoring program over the years, I've worked with many consultants who also provided workshops, facilitation, and other training interventions. The almost insoluble problem for them was that, when they "led" with the training dimension in an organization, they were immediately branded as trainers and/or human resources consultants. Once that happened,

---

[2]That is, they are purchased not primarily for their functionality, which is to move people from one place to another, but rather for the statement they make to others about the owner.

[3]Heaven help us all if *Consumer Reports* decides to do an "objective" set of tests on the consulting industry, as it does for dishwashers and rug cleaners.

the executives refused to consider them for higher level strategy or coaching work. However, if they began their project with strategy or coaching at senior levels, it was relatively easy to segue into training whenever required, because in that case they were branded as the consultants of choice to the executives.

Branding will often occur with or without your help. There is often a default position, and it's rarely good. Your competition, the economy, soured clients, misconceptions, and other factors can create a negative brand. Just as in life, in which failure is the default position (there are really only "causes" of success), a negative image or brand will usually be the default position. You must proactively and aggressively establish a positive and leading-edge brand.

> Branding will occur by default, whether you intend it to or not. Therefore, it's imperative to create the brand that will provide the maximum possible marketing benefit. To believe this to be unimportant is equivalent to believing that your attire or letterhead is unimportant.

Let's understand the difference between deliberate, constructive branding, and default branding (and poor branding). Here are some "real world lessons" we can use to create a road map on the branding journey.

## REAL WORLD LESSONS

Here are some positive and negative brand impacts, which should give us all cause for pause:

*Coca-Cola.* Despite a kind of peculiar taste and the removal of the cocaine that made it such a hit when first invented, Coke has managed to retain one of the strongest brands in the world, uniformly and universally, despite management problems, bottler rebellion, and cut-throat competition. "New Coke" caused a consumer revolt because, emotionally, people could not stand to see their beloved brand disappear. (In blind taste tests, even the most ardent supporters of the original formula couldn't tell the difference between it and New

I had just arrived at a new client for my first few days of onsite work and dreaded meeting the human resource people, who I was sure were going to resent my presence in what they would perceive as their sandbox. Word had apparently leaked out that I was being paid about $150,000 for this project.

Instead, I was met with hearty good cheer and sincere offers of help, not to mention a semi-permanent office and place to hang my hat. I told them, candidly, that I was surprised by the reception.

They told me that, at long last, since I was being paid so well, the executives would have to listen to me, and they were sure that I would reach the same conclusions that they had in human resources. I was simply too high profile, too expensive, and, hence, too credible, to ignore.

My brand was simply superior to theirs, although our expertise and advice were virtually identical.

---

Coke. This was passionate embrace of a brand—a perception—and not a product quality issue at all.)

*Lesson One:* Branding is about passion, emotion, and visceral impulse, not about cold, hard facts.

***Miller Beer.*** Miller at one point had a very powerful brand message: "It's Miller Time!" Everyone seemed to buy into the attitude that after a tough job or a long day, it was, indeed, Miller Time. The problem was that people would actually say, "Well, it's Miller Time. Let's have a Bud!"

*Lesson Two:* The action that must be generated by the brand association is a purchase, not merely an identification or conceptual acknowledgment.

***Jaguar.*** For many years, Jaguar was associated with poor quality, electrical systems that wouldn't be tolerated in a Lionel Train layout, and other bizarre eccentricities usually associated with drafty English estates northeast of Suffolk-on-the-Heather. The company finally went broke (it is now owned by Ford). Jaguar had become a laughing stock among knowledgeable automobile people and a common foil for comics.

*Lesson Three:* A negative brand image that arises by default from ineptitude or incompetence can be almost impossible to overcome.

***Southwest Airlines.*** This "upstart" quickly usurped market share from larger carriers with a no-frills but absolutely on-time and courteous service. Customers would laugh at the lack of amenities and gladly act like cattle to board the planes because they *believed* that the airline would do everything humanly possible to get them to their destination at the time promised. This treatment didn't appeal to the executive traveler who preferred a large seat and a free drink or two, but it wasn't meant to.

*Lesson Four:* Brands do not have to be all things to all people. It's important to identify exactly which buyers you want to appeal to.

***Disney.*** While Walt Disney was alive, he was synonymous with youth-oriented, clean, imaginative entertainment. Disney programs on television and in the movies could be trusted for those attributes (people didn't read reviews of Disney productions to determine whether or not to watch them). The theme parks were famous for meticulous attention to guests' needs, cleanliness, and high value. Today, the Disney Company management has blurred this image, with subsidiaries producing controversial adult films, very public lawsuits with former executives, and escalating prices at its attractions.

*Lesson Five:* When you develop a brand, it must serve as a template for future actions and present conduct; otherwise you create a cognitive dissonance with the public—you say one thing but do another.

> Branding is really about elitism. That is, the buyer should believe that the product or service is uniquely beneficial to his or her condition at that time.

***Miss Piggy.*** Individuals can be a brand unto themselves, even if they're puppets. Miss Piggy, the most aggressive and obtrusive of the Muppet cast, is beloved because she is consistent, outrageous, vain, and strong. She is a little of what a lot of us would probably like to be. She is granted a tolerance and a permission by her Muppet colleagues and by the audience, despite her over-the-top behavior.

*Lesson Six:* Branding isn't about love or affection or even stellar conduct. It's about acceptance under the conditions that bring buyer and seller together.

*NRA.* The National Rifle Association has a duality of brands, depending on the orientation of the observer. For some, it is the repository of constitutional protection and resistance to the oppression of a bureaucratic government. To others, it is the epitome of unjustified trumpeting of individual rights over the good of the public at large. Two different people, observing the exact same brand images, can have two radically different perceptions.

*Lesson Seven:* A powerful brand can repel as many people at it attracts, which is fine so long as it is oriented to attract your buyer and repel non-buyers.

*The U.S. Marines.* The Marines have always branded the corps as one of tough fighters who take on the worst of the battle conditions. But its relatively recent brand statement that they want simply "a few good men" is nothing less than brilliant. In other words, feel free to come to us, but then we'll decide whether you're good enough. If only the postal service had the same brand mentality.

*Lesson Eight:* Brands are seldom as effective when they are egalitarian and available to everyone as they are when "select" and elite and accessible only to those with superior taste/ability/circumstances/intelligence. Such branding doesn't actually discriminate, but merely creates the perception of elitism.

*The Maytag Repairman.* The notion of this poor guy never having anything to do because the product never breaks down is simply brilliant. This is branding "through the back door," insofar as the product quality is touted by informing the consumer that *after the sale* the decision will prove to have been one that eliminates an annoying problem.

*Lesson Nine:* A brand doesn't have to refer directly to a tangible, but can very effectively refer to a set of buyer results that are dramatically attractive.

*MiracleGro.* This is plant food with a great name. I can't even tell you the name of another product that helps in the garden. The name is simply so appropriate and dramatic that it's hard to forget, even if you have no garden. I've always liked this because it hits you right between the eyes.

*Lesson Ten:* A rose by any other name, a brand by any other name, would not smell or sound as sweet. There are times when the name says it all.

These lessons will be applied throughout our discussions in this book.

They constitute a road map of what to pursue and what to avoid in an intelligent branding strategy.

In Chapter 9—which you can certainly preview now, since there's no need to read this book in sequence—we'll talk about the trends that will shape the future and how branding can improve your condition. For the moment, bear in mind that you have to do the worst kind of hard work in your branding, worse than getting your hands dirty or straining your back: You're going to have to think hard and long about your uniqueness and about how you want to convey that to your prospects. That's why a "road map" is important, but you still have to travel the path.

Look behind virtually any strong personal services brand, from Tom Peters to Chicken Soup for just about anything, and you'll find consultants and authors who engaged in some very heavy mental lifting. My intent is to help you get in shape to do that lifting without hurting yourself.

## POSITIONING A BRAND SO THAT THE BRAND POSITIONS YOU

You don't have to be or seek to be number one in your specialty, client base, or geography in terms of size. What you do need is to have a brand that helps to make you number one in whatever niche or manifestation you choose to be seen.

There is a woman known as The Telephone Doctor. Her name is Nancy Friedman, although I have to confess that I had to look that up. I simply know that I can find The Telephone Doctor listed in most training directories, and that when clients have asked me about help with call response centers, interoffice communications, and general phone courtesy, I'm always prompted to cite her firm, although I've never met her and am not familiar with her work.

Assuming there are other people who react as I do, that's a rather fabulous brand because it moves unknown third parties to reference her as a likely resource. That brand works well for anything related to phone use. But I wouldn't recommend her for team building or strategy work, because, for me, the brand precludes those competencies. If, indeed, Ms. Friedman wants to corner the "telephonic skills" market, then she has been quite successful with her brand. If, on the other hand, she wished to offer a full range of organizational consulting services, the brand wouldn't support her well.

You can create and perpetuate many brands. Think of each one as representing a different, unique blend of competency, market need, and passion combined.

Here's one way to determine how many and what kind of brands may suit you. I think this is always a personal, introspective decision, and not one based on the competition or the economy.

As you see in Figure 1.1, three paths must converge:

1. There must be a market need that exists or that you can create. We know that there will always be a market need in our profession for decision making, team building, and compensation consulting, for example. However, in recent years we've also seen attempts to create need (successful and unsuccessful) in terms of executive coaching, life balance, and stress reduction.
2. You must have the competency—or be able to acquire the competency—to meet those market needs. Your set of skills, or those of other resources you employ, must be aligned with fulfilling the customer's needs.
3. You must be passionate about what you do. Branding requires that you believe and act as if you're the best alternative. FedEx bragged about "absolutely, positively getting the package there the next day," not "more often than not getting it there as quickly as we can and barring unforeseen circumstances."

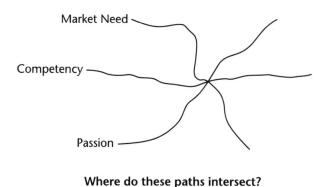

**Where do these paths intersect?**

**Figure 1.1.** Three Converging Paths to Establish Brands

Where these three paths converge, you have the makings of a brilliant brand (or brands—you can identify multiple market needs, develop or acquire numerous competencies, and become passionate in a variety of areas).

Another way to view this is in Figure 1.2.

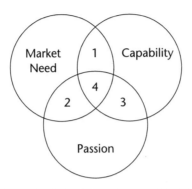

**Figure 1.2.**   Another View of the Three Paths

In position 1, there is a need and you have the competence, but you don't have the passion. There may be a need for better time management skills, and you have several excellent techniques to improve such skills, but it's a boring topic, you've done it before, and it doesn't excite you. (You often see subcontractors in this position, earning their daily bread, but unexcited about the larger project because they don't own it.)

> Branding is as much about passion as it is about the customer's needs. But both are needed. Too many consultants have a beloved methodology that has one drawback: No one else is interested in it.

In position 2, there is a need and you'd love to fill it, but you don't have the ability and/or the capacity. For example, organizations desperately need improved eCommerce skills, you love the Internet, but you don't have the combination of web skills and marketing savvy to pull this off. (This is where you often see incompetent consultants, who talk their way into a job and demonstrate great enthusiasm, but then cannot deliver.)

In position 3, you have the ability and the passion, but no one cares. You are fascinated and enthralled by outdoor experiences, you have mountaineering and orienteering skills and are certified to lead such experiences, but the market has disappeared and no one is interested any longer. (Here you encounter the "messianic" consultants who are fervently pitching their "message," which no one cares about any longer. Think of "right brain/left brain" learning.)

Only in position 4, where all three conditions exist, are you ready, willing, and able to establish a brand and strong marketing gravity around it.

## WHY CONSULTANTS NEED TO GET THEIR HANDS DIRTY IN THE BRANDING BUSINESS

When I was doing the research for an earlier book,[4] I found that a palm reader on the boardwalk of Atlantic City actually required more licensing and certifications than a consultant in mid-town New York. The best thing about the consulting business is that anyone can get into it. The worst thing about the consulting business is . . . well, you guessed it.

This is not a profession that carries a great deal of endemic respect, and it's made worse by the fact that it's totally unregulated. Hence, good consultants need to separate themselves from those between jobs, those who are just dabbling, moonlighting college professors, and the generally inept. (My rule of thumb is that about 50 percent of the people claiming to be consultants actually do not know what they're doing and have no methodology or even operating philosophy.)

In addition to the lack of licensing bodies, the associations representing consultants are extremely weak. The body representing the larger firms (once ACME and now AFME—not exactly memorable) has no muscle or recognition whatsoever; and the largest body representing solo practitioners and smaller firms (IMC—Institute of Management Consultants) has been so beset with financial, organizational, and ego problems that its own members laugh at it. It does provide some value at the local chapter level, but nothing in terms of

---

[4]*Million Dollar Consulting* (McGraw-Hill).

national lobbying, image, education, and so on. These bodies often bestow peculiar sets of initials as a "certification" (for example, "Certified Management Consultant" or CMC), but no buyer in twenty-six years has ever, ever asked me about those credentials.

When you combine three issues, which are not likely to change any time soon, you'll see why we need to create our own brands:

1. Consulting as a profession is not looked on with much respect, is the butt of quite a few jokes, and has been demeaned by a lack of standards to an absence of barriers to entry into the field.
2. There are no effective national organizations providing an umbrella brand or image. The American Bar Association, for example, invests millions to improve the image of lawyers (no easy task), and the American Institute of Architects has created a strong cachet with its "AIA" designation, even though it basically means that a member has simply paid the dues.
3. The larger firms, through sheer bulk and budget, have begun to dominate the media with their advertising, articles, and other promotional strategies.

The average buyer is besieged with messages (particularly true in the United States) about products and services to consider. There are thousands of attempted interventions a day seeking the buyers' focus and attention. There is also a huge proliferation of consulting services, ranging from moonlighting professors to training firms, from huge generalist operations to tiny specialized shops. Ironically, as the big firms merge into fewer entities, the number of consulting "voices" has proliferated.

The differentiation among those services is low. That is, consulting is often dealing with amorphous issues that fall into "lumps" of categories, such as team building, communications, shareholder value, knowledge management, and so on. This is not like deciding that you want to buy a Lincoln and consequently head for that showroom to test drive one. Finally, the Internet has made global marketing available for everyone on virtually any budget. There are seldom even geographies that can be carved out as sacrosanct, let along market niches or business types.

The good news is that the field is wide open. The bad news is that the field is wide open.

## THE PAYOFF OF A STRONG BRAND IN CONSULTING

Those are some of the negatives of not having a strong brand. The positives of a consultant with a strong brand are threefold:

1. You will be able to attract new business with a greater "gravity" (see Chapter 3) than your competition. You should be seen like a laser through the fog of choices above.
2. You will be able to retain your current clients much better, because the buyers will have a stronger sense of who you are and what you can provide in the future. (Your good works will eventually fade in the general chaos of corporate life, but your repute and image tend to live on if firmly established.)
3. You will have a clear template for yourself to tell you what kinds of resources to invest in, what kind of people to hire or subcontract with, what your promotional materials should look like, and so on. A brand is as valuable to your own guidance system as it is for the customer's radar screen. There is a substantial cost-effectiveness that ensues from supporting your brands and being able to eliminate the superfluous and peripheral.

> Branding increases the value proposition. The more you are recognizable, the more you are differentiated, the more potential value you present in the eyes of the buyer. If you're the "only one" who represents that brand, you cannot be a commodity.

Branding can enable you to penetrate markets otherwise dominated by others. Earlier in the chapter I alluded to the old bromide that "no purchasing manager ever was fired for buying IBM." That failed to be true through Big Blue's troubled years, but since then you could say that "no one ever was fired for using FedEx" or "for buying software from Microsoft."

Consultants who establish a successful practice need to brand that success no less than a rancher needs to brand the cattle. You must create ownership that can be identified by the public for your approaches, because in an

For years in my youth, I thought that all film was sold in yellow boxes by some kind of government regulation or industry norm. Of course, it was only Kodak film in those boxes, but Kodak so dominated the industry that I mistook its brand *for the industry.* Only later did I learn about the other film makers, and that was after Kodak had ineptly surrendered much of its market.

You want to be synonymous with your services. The "color of the box" for those competencies ought to be yours. That's brilliant branding.

undifferentiated profession, everything will blend together unless you take the time to differentiate what is yours. Remember when the Boston Consulting Group articulated its four-quadrant strategy model with the star, dog, and so forth? Everyone got busy trying to analyze their own operations using BCG's model. That move effectively cut into the strategy positions of all other firms, including McKinsey's.

Consultants need brands because brands enable the consultant to improve the value proposition that the buyer perceives, thereby enhancing the ability of the consultant to establish and close large, comprehensive contracts.

## THE ULTIMATE SECRET OF BRANDING

You'll know from my prior books[5] that I perceive *value* to be the primary determinant of contribution to the client, and the basis for fees. Consultants should base their fees on their contribution to the value of the project for the client organization.

Consequently, the true secret of branding is to establish your brand based on the value that the client will receive. Brands should be about improving the client condition, not about how good you are. When Mercedes claimed it was

---

[5]For example, *Million Dollar Consulting* and *The Ultimate Consultant* (Jossey-Bass).

"engineered like no other car in the world," it was also implicitly stating that you were safer in it, more comfortable in it, and looked better in it. Kodak's best branding ever occurred when it talked not about its film or its cameras, but about the customers' memories.

The best consultants don't talk about surveys, coaching, focus groups, competitive analysis, or any of the other methodologies that they might employ. They talk instead about the client's increase in market share, better communications, retention of top talent, and public image. If we've established that no one buys a drill because he wants a drill, but rather because he needs a hole somewhere, then we can be absolutely sure that no one retains a consultant because she needs a consultant (or even a focus group or a training program). What the buyer needs is improved morale, larger sales per person, a safer plant, and a more competitive compensation system.

So, before you move on through the book, let's establish at the outset that branding is more effective *when it represents some improved condition for the customer,* such as getting my package "absolutely, positively" somewhere the next day. The sequence is presented in Figure 1.3. (You're entitled to one complicated chart, and this is it.)

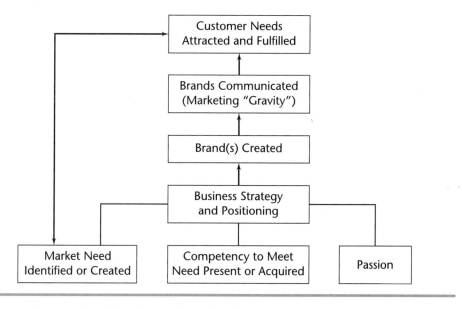

**Figure 1.3.** Basing Brands on Value to the Customer

We established earlier that your business strategy will be most viable and effective when based on a combination of market need, competency, and passion. That positioning will enable you to create a brand (or brands—I want to emphasize that multiple brands are clearly feasible and even preferable). The key is then to create a communications strategy to attract people to your brand, which I call the marketing "gravity."

The customer is then attracted to those brands that have been especially created to cater to his or her needs. The assessment of market need and the nature of the brand create a dynamic that should be constantly examined and fine-tuned. Mercedes gave up "engineered like no other car in the world" after a decade, because it realized that its buyers also wanted a personal sensation, not one of cold, Teutonic engineering prowess alone. Brands wax and wane as market needs change.

---

Branding always starts with customer need, or need you can create for the customer. Everyone knows that you know how good you are. The point, however, is: How good are you for them?

---

Before we conclude, let's take a look at your current brand potential. By the end of the book, you might significantly change your mind, but it will be helpful to have some examples in mind as we proceed through the process, and this will make it as personal as possible.

Here's a template to determine what your brands might be. If you already have brands, you can test them.

A. Cite four competencies you are especially proficient at (for example, facilitating retreats, analyzing competitive positions, and so forth):

1. _____

2. _____

3. _____

4. _____

B. Circle those about which you are passionate (for example, you take so much gratification in the work that you would do it for free). You may circle as many as you wish.

C. Cite four market needs for *any two competencies* you've circled (for example, greater sales velocity for a client would be addressed by your own competency for developing leads into clients).

Competency 1:

1. _____

2. _____

3. _____

4. _____

Competency 2:

1. _____

2. _____

3. _____

4. _____

D. Write down the brands that you already have or that you could create to match those market needs and competencies above (for example, "The Sales Accelerator" might match the prior example).

1. _____

2. _____

3. _____

4. _____

E. Final step: Write down the communications devices (the "gravity") you currently have in place for *any* of those brands (for example, a weekly column, a
website featuring the brands, speaking engagements, products, and so forth).

1. _____

2. _____

3. _____

4. _____

5. _____

6. _____

7. _____

8. _____

As you'll see in Chapter 3, there are a lot more elements to gravity than
merely eight devices, but if you have that many in place, then you're already
ahead of the game. Yet my work with consultants indicates that not many go
through even this simple exercise. They seem to believe that, if they are fortu-
nate with the right clients and word-of-mouth takes over, then they will be
"branded." That's really the viewpoint of the cattle, not the rancher, and the cattle are the ones for whom branding is painful, as I think I've read somewhere,
being a kid from New York.

> You have to wield the branding iron. You can't wait for the world to
> brand you. It's too slow, too erratic, and always quite painful.

## BRAND NEW LESSONS

Consultants need a brand because the public—and the buyers—have no particular clarity on the profession or its practitioners, other than a sometimes negative one. This is a largely undifferentiated business, in which monolithic firms

have the loudest voices and the biggest footprints. Branding must always be based on the buyer's perception of value to him or her or to the organization.

In the following chapters we'll discuss how to build brands with a variety of specific tactics. We've tried here, however, to convince you that it is necessary. If you don't believe that, then the following chapters probably won't be of too much help in an overall branding strategy, although they will provide plenty of specific options for communicating your value.

However, the importance of effective branding is that, once established, the brands remain in place, constantly attracting new business in the most cost-effective way imaginable. They are perpetual marketing devices requiring only occasional maintenance and fine-tuning.

As a consultant, you don't need a brand to survive. But you do need a brand to thrive.

# CHAPTER 2

# You Don't Start at the Beginning

## *You Have the Makings of a Brand at Hand*

This "Top Gun" series of books is focused on the successful consultant. If you are in that demographic, you probably have created the recipe for one or more brands merely through the dint of your success over the years. (If you don't fit that demographic, read on, because you'll learn what to put in place as you gain clients and momentum that will establish brands for you all the more quickly.)

### IDENTIFYING THE INGREDIENTS OF YOUR BRANDS

There are two primary sources for determining the elements of your brands that may already exist:

1. Those traits and attributes that you've tended to emphasize and support in your promotional materials, publishing, speaking, and discussions with prospects

2. Those results and accomplishments for which existing clients have tended to laud you and provide testimonials

Of these two sources, the second is by far the most important. That's because they provide a view "from the outside in," meaning that others who support your work attribute these abilities as the reason they have happily invested in your help. In other words, the perspective is from the position of those very buyers and organizations that you want to appeal to as future clients in your marketing plans.

This is a vital separation of criteria (your perspective versus your clients') because we're all fooled much too easily. At one point I was delivering a speech to four hundred outstanding small business owners at an awards banquet and the crowd responded with overwhelming enthusiasm to my "four points for every small business." At the conclusion of the night, I was told that I was the finest speaker that the group had seen in its fifteen years of existence and awards nights.

"Come on," I said with false modesty, "I'm sure I'm not the very best of all those speakers."

"Oh, but you are," gushed the program chair. "Everyone is talking about your performance."

"Well," I said, unable to resist, "what did you particularly enjoy about it?"

"Why, we've never had anyone here who could hold a microphone, walk around the stage, and speak all at the same time!"

"What about my four points for small business?" I stuttered.

"What four points?" she asked.

---

Brand elements should be examined in terms of what has attracted someone to you, not what attracts you to yourself.

## RECIPE: FINDING THE RIGHT RAW MATERIALS AND MIXTURES

To ensure that you begin on the path of least resistance—with those attributes that your clients already tend to associate with you as valuable to them—use this checklist to assemble potential brands or their elements:

- *Is there a pattern to your testimonial letters?* Do the testimonial letters and even informal notes of thanks tend to refer to a common theme, such as the rapidity with which you built teams or your ability to resolve conflict in a constructive manner?
- *Have referrals cited common reasons for contacting you?* Do prospects who reach out to you from third-party endorsements mention a unifying reason, such as an affinity for both executives and front-line managers, or multi-cultural sensitivity?
- *Has your marketing gravity[1] generated a particular kind of interest?* Do your marketing efforts create an attraction for prospects in a common area, such as sales acceleration or expert witness work?
- *What speech content has tended to draw the largest audiences, most repeat performances, and/or the best reactions from the participants?* Are there paid or free speeches and talks that have used particular themes which the audiences and/or organizers have requested the most often and reacted to with the most enthusiasm and follow-up?
- *What articles or interviews have generated the easiest placement, most requests for additional material, and/or best follow-up?* Have you published items around certain topics or issues that have been easiest to place, or that have actually been requested of you by editors and interviewers?
- *Do you have products that sell far better than others?* Are there manuals, booklets, charts, or other job aids that are exceedingly popular? (This takes on extra weight if the item is among the most expensive that you sell, meaning that the interest overcomes price sensitivity.)[2]
- *Do certain pages on your website attract far more "hits" than any others?* Are there content-driven aspects of your site (that is, apart from free offers and other inducements) that generate more interest for visitors than others?
- *What do client surveys tell you?* Do your clients provide a pattern of results, outcomes, or general improvement as a result of your services? (If you

---

[1]See the following chapter for "gravity" specifics.

[2]For example, one of my most expensive items among thirty products is a $149 book entitled *How to Write a Proposal That's Accepted Every Time.* I know that proposal writing has to be one of my brands because of its immense popularity. So "The Value Priced Sale and the Perfect Proposal" has become a brand and the title of a cassette album.

don't utilize client surveys, a branding strategy is a good justification for beginning them.)

- *What do you hear when you network or socialize with colleagues?* Do people who have just met you say, "You're the consultant who's known for changing images overnight," for example? Or are you introduced to others by people who know you as, "This is the person who creates high-profit customer call centers"?

Use the template above to determine what common themes and unifying attributes are associated *with the results that you've generated.* This view "from the outside in" will be the most rapid, dramatic, accurate, and highest potential "lure" for creating brands that will appeal to similar buyers in new organizations.[3] The odds are that you have a great deal of material that can lead to successful branding, but you don't have it manifest or organized in the proper manner that reveals its true power.

> Branding must be built on repetitive and distinctive abilities and accomplishments that can be replicated. If you can't duplicate it, or if it isn't sufficiently distinguishing, it's an isolated incident and not a brand, no matter how successful at the time.

Finally, note that we are constantly talking about "themes" and "patterns." Don't allow a single success, no matter how grand, with a particular client to lead you to believe you have a brand in that area. By definition, brands must be apparent and appealing to a range of buyers, even in narrow markets. Consequently, a singular success may be so unique that its appeal does not transcend that organization or even that brief window in time when you worked with that client. Many consultants have made the mistake of trying to parlay a single suc-

---

[3]Note that this is an excellent process if you want to build brands on current success. But if you choose to build brands that lead you in new directions (for example, you've been highly successful in the low-paying human resources and training areas but want to move into line management consulting), then you need to reorganize your image. We'll cover this process later in this chapter.

I was approached by a woman during a workshop for consultants who was dressed in stylish army fatigues—camouflage—which has become all the rage. She said, "I've thought about it a long time, and I don't have a brand that I can identify. Can you help? I'll pay whatever it takes."

Despite a flash of mercenary mayhem, I asked why she dressed like that, and what her consulting specialty or field was. She told me that she focused on creating organizational change among those who thought it hopeless—companies being outclassed by the competition, old "brick and mortar" shops, employees who felt incapable of improvement, businesses in tough markets.

As for her outfit, she was the first woman paratrooper in the 82nd Airborne Division, one of the very first at West Point, where she finished first in her class, and held several other distinctions that made my eyes pop.

"You're the change commando," I joked. Then we looked at each other for a few seconds, and she went scurrying back to her seat to begin writing her new marketing materials.

I wonder how much she would have paid. . . .

cess into a brand, when the success may be more due to the client's situation, the timing, or even luck (which even the best of us desperately need and pray for on occasion) than due to any distinguishing consultant attribute.

I once was part of a "virtual consulting team," consisting of one other independent consultant with whom I had never before worked and an internal consultant from the client company. We were able to beat one of the "big five" consulting organizations for a major, six-figure project by building on the "virtual" brand and demonstrating how our unique blend of external savvy and internal presence were just right for a restructuring project. We never even attempted to duplicate that again, and I've never found the conditions elsewhere that would allow me to attempt it.

Some unique successes are simply that, and not necessarily conducive to building a brand. That's why the search for repetitive perceptions, trends, and commonality is so important.

Some overall criteria for what patterns to include as potentially brand-worthy:

- Originate with your best, largest, and longest term customers (Go with the strongest flow)
- Can be replicated by you, alone, without unique assistance or conditions (Brands shouldn't be reliant on other resources)
- Appeal to the widest possible array of potential buyers (Get the most bang for your buck, as the fireworks people are fond of saying)
- Are configured or labeled uniquely enough to set you apart from the competition (Established brands are very difficult to displace)
- Represent, in your view, future market needs, competencies that you will continually improve, and your continued passion, as cited in the prior chapter on the convergence of these three factors (Don't pursue a brand in which you will lose interest, ability, or market need)
- Are resistant to trends, fads, technology leaps, and other uncontrollable forces (Try to assert maximum control over your brands)
- Are not capital intensive (You want to maximize ROI)
- Can be readily defended, and might be trademarked, patented, copyrighted, and protected in other manners, legally and ethically (A great brand that is usurped is a very bad misfortune)
- Provide for minimal brand competition with larger firms or with brands firmly established in the field (You might make a great cola, but that's not a market that's going to provide either high margins or decent market share without getting bloody)

---

Once you've understood your brand potential, you have to help others to understand their actuality. Those are two vastly different endeavors.

## MAGNIFYING YOUR EXISTING REPUTE

Once you've isolated those accomplishments that lead to branding, you can begin to magnify them, which is what you've really just done for yourself and now must do for others. You might look at it this way:

How to Establish a Unique Brand in the Consulting Profession

Your brands already exist, but they have not been sufficiently emphasized or accentuated (probably not even for yourself prior to this exercise). You need to bring a magnifier or amplifier to bear in order to provide more visibility and awareness for prospects.

First, you have to decide what levels of branding you wish to pursue. These levels are not mutually exclusive, and some organizations engage in all of them. But the level you choose will make a difference in terms of the type and range of magnification you apply.

*Corporate Branding.*   This brand embraces your firm or practice as an entity and will build on that name. McKinsey has become a brand, as has Boston Consulting Group (and then BCG).[4] The gamut of organizational abilities and potential is encompassed in a corporate brand. The key buying questions that corporate level branding answers are:

- Is this a trustworthy and reliable organization?
- Is this a legitimate and solid firm?

*Advantages:* One size fits all, and the corporate brand, if successful, can be used for all of your promotion and market impact. It is a single focus that is most easily promoted. You've probably seen full-page, strategic ads placed for the likes of Andersen Consulting toward this end.

*Disadvantages:* Smaller firms, and certainly solo practitioners, seldom have the worth of what they've done represented by the company name. Also, corporate branding is best done in conjunction with other levels of branding, in that solely corporate branding is most successful when the offerings of the firm are narrow and fixed. It's tough to be "all things to all people" if your firm

---

[4]One of the features of corporate branding is that a "shorthand" or initials may result, demonstrating the power of the reference. Federal Express, for instance, legally changed its name to FedEx, because that is the brand name that the market developed for it. Go with the most powerful flow.

attempts to use a single corporate brand but actually has a diversity of offerings and potential for the client. The buyer generally will associate you with a single image.

> Branding can occur at a variety of levels and emphases. This is an organic process, and you can build additional levels over time without threatening prior work if you plan carefully.

*Unifying Branding.* This is a common form of branding, which features a single brand that is applied to a range of products and/or services. Mercedes provides its names on all of its various models, even trucks, as a unifying brand or marque, as does Fleet Bank or Campbell's Soup.[5] In consulting, the Psychological Press puts its imprimatur across a wide array of test instruments that it creates and/or endorses and distributes, and Towers Perrin provides a variety of compensation and benefit services and reports under its unifying branding.

The questions which unifying branding answers include:

- Are these products and services of equal value and integrity?
- Does this firm offer a diversity of connected services?

*Advantages:* It is relatively easy to connect the services offered to the company offering them, and one brand can accommodate a variety of products and services, making it cost-effective.

*Disadvantages:* A lack of differentiation can easily occur when there is a wide variety of offerings. In other words, the unifying brand "elasticity" must be so wide as to be non-discriminating. It's one thing to encompass all types of Mercedes-Benzes, despite cost, but it's another to attempt to encompass strategy formulation, executive coaching, front-line workshops, and competitive

---

[5]As opposed to Procter & Gamble, which uses differing product names without any unifying identification with the company, or Toyota, which deliberately removes its name from the Lexus line.

analysis. The more you specialize, the more a unifying brand might apply effectively; the more you generalize, the more problematic it becomes.

*Service Group Branding.*   To overcome the disadvantages of too much elasticity noted above, groups of services (or products) can be assembled under a particular brand designation. Lincoln/Mercury is a division of Ford with a particular market niche, advertising, promotion, and well over a dozen unique models. When one sees, say, a Lincoln Navigator SUV, one does not instantly (or, perhaps, ever) think of Ford. Similarly, "shareholder value" is a brand used by some consulting firms[6] to differentiate a range of their services within a larger array of other offerings they provide. Obviously, this strategy enabled a firm or practice to group similar services (even when there is overlap from grouping to grouping) around several distinct brand images.

The questions this approach answers in the marketplace are:

- What are the natural synergies that the offerings provide?
- What is the "universe" within which the services exist?

*Advantages:* Service group branding affords the ability to take virtually unlimited services for the generalist and group them into "specialist" packages, each with a distinct image and recognition factor. The approach prevents the "all things to all people" syndrome often associated with the generalist, and even offers the practitioner who is uncomfortable with such generalizing the ability to more specifically organize offerings and their promotion.

*Disadvantages:* It requires some careful organization married to acceptance of ambiguity to create discrete packages that represent various value propositions, but which may also overlap in places (for example, a 360° feedback technique might apply in both the executive coaching group and in the team-building group). Also, if a key buyer closely identifies you with a particular package without awareness of others, it may be very difficult to broaden that viewpoint, especially and ironically after great success in that single group area.

---

[6]The first firm I heard do this was Braxton Associates in the early 1990s.

All branding levels have pros and cons, which is why it's almost always best to embark on a strategy of multi-level branding. The emphasis here is on "strategy," so that the various levels are mutually supportive.

*Single Service Branding.* This may be perceived as the most common level that we see as consumers, but it is actually on the decline in favor of group branding. The equation is simple: One service (or product), one brand. If you offer only a single, narrow service, the choice is simple. If you offer (as I hope you do) more than that, then multiple brands are called for. You might refer to these as "horizontal brands," since they don't create additional levels but differentiate parallel service and product offerings. There are practitioners who serve only as expert witnesses; there are trainers who provide solely telemarketing seminars for banks; there are turnaround consultants who deal only with family-owned manufacturing businesses of less than $20 million in sales. There are also practitioners who provide a wide range of otherwise unrelated services, and each merits and needs a brand of its own.

The questions answered here are:

- What is the validity and distinction of this particular service?
- What is the degree of specialization in this area?

*Advantages:* This is a very simple technique and easy for the buyer to relate to. "I want some M&Ms" is never confused with "Get me the candy coated chocolate from the Mars Company." Similarly, "Get me The Telephone Doctor™" is far easier than "Find Nancy Friedman, who specializes in phone techniques." You can have a plethora of single service brands providing that kind of focus for potential buyers.

*Disadvantages:* These can create tremendous distraction, loss of focus, and additional expense, unless coordinated in an intelligent combination with other levels of branding. Solo practitioner and small firms (and even large firms) tend to subsume those single-service brands that are not immediately in use, request-

How to Establish a Unique Brand in the Consulting Profession

ed, or favored. (This is why services that are acquired through acquisition are often trampled by the existing strong services and support systems of the acquirer.) These are tough to use in any quantity without broader coordination.

*Note:* Some single products take on a branding force so strong that you have to make changes in the product or service to fully exploit the branding. On the one hand, Kleenex, Formica, and Xerox were all threatened with becoming generic brand names for facial tissue, countertops, and copying (as is FedEx today for overnight shipping), so that "Kleenex brand tissues" had to be amended to the name. More recently, one brand of duct tape actually changed the product name to "Duck Tape" with a picture of a duck on it, because so many people mispronounced the product name that the manufacturer decided it was more profitable to simply go with the flow and exploit the name that the misinformed buyers were actually using.

*Personal Name Branding.* This occurs when you are able to develop a repute about your own name. I don't mean a name that has become generic for a company (such as, McKinsey or Andersen or Merrill Lynch), but rather your name representing your personality and talents. Many consultants who are known for their "smarts," whom people want on retainer, who are known to achieve results ("You need to contact a guy named Alan Weiss for this project before you do anything else") have developed personal name brands. This is an ideal situation, since the promotion of the brand and promotion of yourself are one and the same.

The questions answered in such promotion:

- Why have I heard so much about this person?
- What does his or her name represent in terms of value to me?

*Advantages:* "Find Alan Weiss" is the best form of brand promotion imaginable and creates a "buzz" in the marketplace. Moreover, the brand can't be stolen, duplicated, or impinged on. There is only one you, and you don't have to bolster that with added validity (for example, "We were the first to create the 'balanced scorecard' approach to performance"). You are the only one who is you.

*Disadvantages:* There is a high degree of ambiguity involved, and prospects can quickly lose interest unless you demonstrate rapidly (in print, on the web, and/or in conversation) exactly *why* you're so valuable. There's also the famous "Hollywood phenomenon" that goes like this: "Get me a young Alan Weiss," "Get me an Alan Weiss who knows insurance," "Get me a less expensive Alan Weiss," and so on.

*Note:* If your name has become a brand unto itself, take all necessary actions to build on it and protect it, since you may have used the other branding techniques to create your name recognition, and they are still the "gravity" factors in place. For example, I've taken the domain name "AlanWeiss.com," and if someone tries to find me that way or writes an email to Alan@Alan-Weiss.com, the search and the mail are automatically forwarded to my SummitConsultingGroup.com address and to my email at that address. When I began in the business, no one would have tried to find me that way, since the web wasn't in use to the current degree and neither was my name. Without altering any of my other web "gravity," I've ensured that people trying to find me by this brand name will be directed toward my major source and promotional material.[7]

> Keep your name aligned with whatever you do, so that the chances of your marketing efforts attaching themselves to your name, making it into a brand unto itself, are maximized. The most powerful branding is value associated with merely the mention of your name.

## RE-ENERGIZING YOUR BRAND FOR MAXIMUM IMPACT

We alluded above to the fact that you might want to reorganize your branding efforts now that you've reached this point of success. That's because branding can plateau. A brand can take you on a steep growth curve, but it can level off, as shown in Figure 2.1.

---

[7]If you're interested, there are many sites on the web that can arrange this for you. I used one called NameSecure.com, which charged under $100 for two years of registration, maintenance, and forwarding.

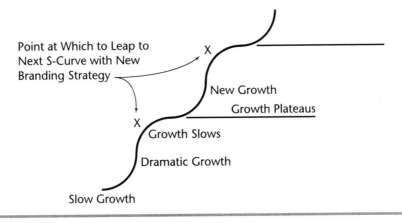

**Figure 2.1.** Avoiding Brand Plateaus

In Figure 2.1, the plateau phenomenon can be seen. Brands do become dated, passé, and copied (legally or illegally). The reasons include:

- The brand is associated with a past event that is no longer deemed modern or current, such as "space age" or "laser-like." In consulting, "shareholder

## VIGNETTE

Poland Spring had been a rather pedestrian purveyor of bottled water. The company focused on home and office use. However, with the advent of the bottled water craze, Poland Spring revitalized itself with bottled water for sale in supermarkets, grocery stores, and even some restaurants. It continues to do what it always has—bottle water from the ground and its proprietary "springs"—but is now reaching a far trendier audience.

When consultants move from an accent on their technology (for example, running change management programs) to an emphasis instead on current buyer needs (for example, creating innovation and positive change in competitive markets), the consultants are taking their regular spring water but bottling it so that it reaches more sophisticated tastes.

Staying current means constantly climbing, not resting on the plateau.

value" and "portfolio management" are two brands that have come and gone. No one wants to go through est any longer.[8]

- The brand has fallen into disrepute. "T-groups" and "left/right brain" thinking were very hot training issues in their time, but have been debunked or demoted in terms of actual utility on the job.

- The brand has become too generic for meaningful attraction. We've cited "It's Miller time, let's have a Bud," and the problems with using a term such as "Xerox" as a verb. "Strategic planning," probably first created and detailed by Peter Drucker during his early work at GM and GE, is no longer a differentiator for a consulting firm.

- Some brands are too easy to copy. Social Style Theory, probably first created by a Dr. Robert Merrill in the 1950s, was since marketed and implemented by a plethora of training firms. There are books out today, albeit not very good ones, that deal exclusively with this approach without ever mentioning the source or originator.

- The brand has established a negativism that is exacerbated by attempts to change it. Oldsmobile, one of the great names in automotive history, has disappeared. GM's attempts to change what it perceived as a stodgy image were focused on "not your father's Oldsmobile," which alienated young and old alike. As buyer demographics change, brands must change, but not at the cost of what has made them popular. (Mercedes, flush with new technology and great designing, still draws on its automotive history in its advertising, which has enabled it to go "down market" with the A class while maintaining the exclusivity of its marque.)

Too often we find words like "new" and "improved" and "better than ever" on the same old products. And that's why consulting firms and academics are continually producing "new" models surrounding strategy, finance, the management of people, and other factors that haven't really changed (for example, "reengineering," the "learning organization," and "knowledge management").

---

[8]For those of you born after the 1970s, Erhard Seminar Training (est) was the brainchild of Werner Erhard (aka Jack Rosenberg) and became a cult-like, draconian self-awareness seminar series that fell out of favor as swiftly as it had arisen.

# FIVE WAYS TO ENSURE BRAND FRESHNESS

If you are seeking to reorganize your branding efforts, or if you fear that you are reaching a plateau, remember that the time to act ideally is prior to reaching the plateau. You want to make the "leap" while you have upward acceleration, not after you've flattened out, which requires more velocity to escape to the next higher level. Never be content with your brand efforts. Always be vigilant for ways to improve on them. Here are five techniques:

1. *Establish Branding Priorities.* From the list above you may decide that one element will be your first priority, another will be secondary, and two others will be tertiary. You can invest time and resources accordingly and, if you see more movement from one tactic than from others, you can "promote" it to a more primary force in your marketing efforts.
2. *Create Niche Brands.* This means that you may have one brand for your insurance consulting business, another for your executive coaching specialty, and a third for your workshops and seminars. They may at times overlap, which is fine. In this way you can build on what you've traditionally been successful in ("The gold standard in agent training") while building potentially wider brands in other areas without diluting the first one and the bread that's already on the table ("America's business coach").[9]
3. *Use the "Private Label" Mentality.* For example, the CVS drug store chain has its own brand of popular over-the-counter medications, less expensive than the more famous brand names. This technique can also be used to denote premium value and premium prices. It's easy and effective to create the "Acme Consulting Small Business Growth Process," for example. I utilize the Alan Weiss Private Roster Mentoring Program, using my brand name to provide cachet and distinction for mentoring, which is in and of itself a widespread, undifferentiated process.
4. *Engage in Co-Branding Efforts.* I have an alliance partner, Kennedy Information, which publishes *Consultant's News, What's Working in Consulting,* and engages in a wide variety of other consulting-related products and

---

[9]I once knew a guy who ran seminars all by himself, but every piece of promotion would cite the fact that he was "personally presenting" that particular seminar on that specific date. It was an interesting approach that cost him nothing.

services. Together we run a seminar series called "Rainmaking: Strategies for Consulting Success," presented by Alan Weiss. These cash in on the Kennedy brand for consulting resources, and my brand for excellent presentations and value-based pricing. Co-mingling our brands creates a powerful synergy. I also publish some of my books through their production company, and edit one of their newsletters. You have seen numerous instances of a product being offered with the admonition that it can also be purchased using a certain credit card, which is another example of effective co-branding.

Brand change or alteration is always best done from a position of strength. Don't examine a brand addition or change strategy as a last resort to weak performance. Examine it regularly as an aggressive strategy for growth.

5. *Broaden or Elasticize the Existing Brand(s). Playboy* used the brand derived from the magazine to embrace products, video, and catalog sales. Everyone from Calvin Klein to Ferrari has tried to stretch existing, high brand recognition, with varying levels of success. If you have some products or services that seem orphaned or are poor performers, consider "embracing" them under one of your successful brands to see whether a synergy will take place. For example, if you are having erratic results with a public speaking career, try billing yourself as "The Strategist" (assuming that your consulting work has flourished there) or as "The Coaches' Coach." If successful, the "orphan" should not only flourish, but should then lend strength to the overall brand, as well.

# THE CRITICAL CASE FOR STRATEGIC BRANDING

As a successful consultant, you have the wherewithal to create effective brands immediately, if you haven't already done so. But brand creation, by intent or by default, is clearly insufficient. You need a brand strategy that coordinates your efforts, maximizes allure, and can evolve as your success continues (and as conditions inevitably change).

Your various brands should, optimally, provide synergy and mutual support. While it's quite acceptable to keep some brands "isolated" so that they appeal to a particular buyer or market or represent a particular talent, it's far better to create a dynamic support among brands. In this way, your strategy supports your competitive intelligence work, which provides speaking opportunities, which create interest in your strategy work, and so on. As a rule of thumb that might make several readers rather irate, the more a brand is neatly isolated with no relationship to the rest of your work, the more likely that it is an avocation or pastime, and not an occupation. I often find consultants with weird, unrelated outcroppings of offerings, such as presentation skills, or overcoming adversity, or facilities management. These are almost always remnants of one's past or a personally interesting diversion, but seldom a major service offering of interest to buyers.

The strategy needn't be complex, but it should be systematic and continually examined for marketing results and potential. One such methodical approach can be seen in Figure 2.2, which is expanded below.

1. Define your strengths *through your clients' eyes.* Don't be content with an assessment of your own abilities or successes. Find out why your clients have hired you, particularly repeat clients and larger clients. Have them explain the reasons in terms of their business outcomes, not that you're simply such a consummate professional. (There are a lot of consummate professionals, but not many who can increase sales by 20 percent, if you get my drift.) I've worked with a person whose entire, lengthy accolades talk about how well he facilitates groups and keeps meetings flowing. That's nice, but not especially breathtaking. We went back to his clients to specify that those same talents actually produced decreased conflict, better teamwork, more productive units, and greater cross-functional collaboration to meet business goals. The former was the basis for a pat on the back; the latter was the basis for a brand.
2. Establish your brands based on those strengths. We've discussed at length the alternatives to creating brands (and in the next chapter we'll talk at length about the tactics to implement them). Dispose of brands that haven't been productive or do not exploit the strengths. Don't be overly modest about being shameless in that promotion. I was recently called

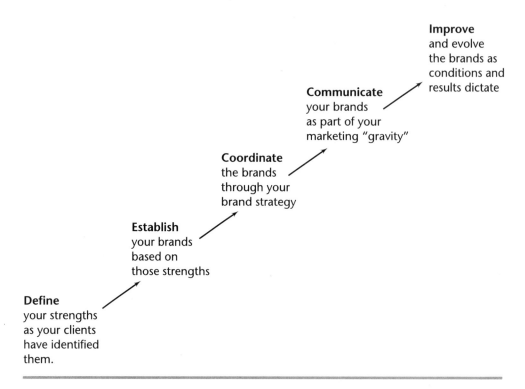

**Improve**
and evolve
the brands as
conditions and
results dictate

**Communicate**
your brands
as part of your
marketing "gravity"

**Coordinate**
the brands
through your
brand strategy

**Establish**
your brands
based on
those strengths

**Define**
your strengths
as your clients
have identified
them.

**Figure 2.2.** A Strategic Approach to Branding

"the rock star of consulting" and immediately began to use it as a brand in certain professional niches. Create as many brands as your comfort level, business planning, and repute will allow.

3. Coordinate the brands through the brand strategy discussed earlier. Ideally, create a synergy so that brands can support each other and embrace otherwise "orphaned" elements of the business. Make sure that none is contradictory. Confine some to certain markets and certain usage, and broaden others so that they virtually always accompany your name. Be clear on their priorities and what you intend to invest in each.

4. Communicate your brands as part of your marketing "gravity." This is the subject of the next chapter, the tactics that will implement your strategy. Brands cannot be passive and do you no good if dormant. They must be an integral aspect of your promotion and image. Ironically, their ability to attract is reinforced by their ability to attract. In other words, "Get me Alan Weiss, the mentoring expert," becomes simply "Get me Alan

Weiss." The success of the attraction solidifies the simplicity and power of the brand.

5. Improve and evolve the brands as conditions and results dictate. You want to avoid the plateaus and take advantage of the upward acceleration. Be prepared to "leap" to the next S-curve of brand growth and attraction. The best way to avoid the competition or keep the constantly changing times from undermining your branding efforts is to be constantly on the lookout to improve them yourself. At the very least, schedule a twice-a-year review of your brands and branding strategy with your trusted advisors or another, non-competing consultant.

---

Branding strategy and marketing strategy are inextricably linked. You cannot—and should not—perform one without the other.

## BRAND NEW LESSONS

You don't have to start at square zero. You probably have brands, or the potential for brands, clearly established by virtue of your past successes. Your challenge is to isolate what the most powerful potential is in terms of your own business strategy and to coordinate and invest in those that will provide the most acceleration toward your business plans.

To establish that future, you first have to take a look back, with the help of clients, to determine what client results best symbolize your talents and contributions.

The ultimate brand is your name. As your brands mutually reinforce each other and create synergy, a key goal should be to make your name synonymous with your intended market strategy, or simply with excellence in your field. Build on this with effective and relentless communications. You want the buyer to say, "Get me that Sharon Smith," not "Get me, oh, what's her name. . . ?"

# CHAPTER 3

# The Gravity of Brands: Creating Irresistible Attraction

## Using Brands to Draw Buyers to You

Brands are attention-getting devices. You can think of them as creating magnetism, attraction, or allure. I like to think of them as creating a gravitation field that draws prospects to you, hence, the term I created about five years ago is "marketing gravity." I've chosen this metaphor because gravity is *always present*. It needn't be turned on or off, requires no maintenance, and the larger the mass the more gravity exerted.

The more gravity you create, the more that the gravity will build on itself, so that the attractive force becomes exponential in its growth, not linear.

In Figure 3.1 various gravity elements are represented. You might already be employing additional ones, or various derivations of these. There is nothing magic about the numbers or types depicted, except that they represent the elements that I've

**Creating Marketing Gravity**

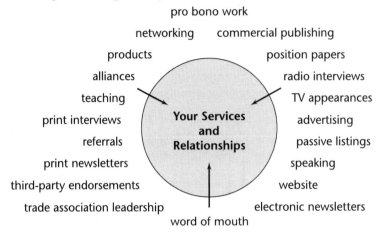

pro bono work

networking   commercial publishing

products   position papers

alliances   radio interviews

teaching   TV appearances

print interviews   **Your Services and Relationships**   advertising

referrals   passive listings

print newsletters   speaking

third-party endorsements   website

trade association leadership   electronic newsletters

word of mouth

**Figure 3.1.** Elements of Marketing Gravity

established for myself during my career. That doesn't mean that they are the best, only that I know for a fact that they can all be created by one person, and that they can all be supported simultaneously.

Some simple rules for gravity elements follow:

- You can create and maintain as many or as few as your comfort level allows.
- These are high priority time investments, so the old refrain "I don't have enough time" would be like saying "I don't have enough time to talk to a prospective client." In that case, something is wrong with you, not with the model.
- I always advise that you choose some elements well within your comfort level and a few outside of it, since you'll otherwise be restricted to certain narrow marketing avenues. Market need, not personal comfort, should be addressed by your elements.
- Don't expect "quick hits," such as numbers of calls after an article or daily visits to a website. These are cumulative devices, not ambushes.
- You only need one good response. I've had friends brag about 20,000 responses, only to be unable to qualify them and generate absolutely no business from them. Conversely, I've been running one inexpensive ad for

    How to Establish a Unique Brand in the Consulting Profession

ten years that has resulted in only one piece of business thus far. It was for $156,000, all profit.

- As many elements should be leveraged as possible. In other words, position papers can also be posted on a website, and pro bono work can lead to news releases.

All marketing elements are accelerated by a brand that is attractive, recognizable, and uniquely associated with you. Branding is the fusion that drives successful marketing.

- You are far better off with fewer elements that are unique and distinguishing, rather than with many elements that are run-of-the-mill. Of course, you're best off with many elements that are unique and distinguishing.

# VIGNETTE

I was at a human resource conference and the speaker was putting the crowd to sleep. Oblivious, he charged ahead with his convoluted models and unimpressive examples.

"This is painful," I said to the meeting's coordinator.

"Yes," she admitted, "he's like this every year."

"EVERY YEAR?" I nearly shouted. "Why on earth to you invite him back?"

"His work appears everywhere, his name is known by everyone, and he's a big draw. Even the feedback from this event will be positive because people believe it was their fault for 'not getting it,' and not his for not presenting it well."

I guess even Ming the Merciless[1] had his own powerful brands.

---

[1]Okay, for those of you who are too young, Ming was the villain through the entire Flash Gordon movie series.

Your marketing gravity should revolve around communicating your brand to potential buyers specifically and the public-at-large generally. Let's examine how that's done.

## THE ELEMENTS THAT CREATE GRAVITATIONAL ATTRACTION

There is no priority in general among these elements, although you might find that some will be more important than others for you. I'll discuss them as if each were equal, but I'll also describe why some may be more powerful than others. For those of you who desire some starting points, I've placed an asterisk after those elements that I consider "musts" for successful brand strategies. We'll start at 12 o'clock and work our way around.

### Pro Bono Work

This is an exceptionally powerful device for newcomers to the profession or for aggressive marketing within the profession. It is also a terrific approach for people who prefer to work locally and stay off airplanes, or for reformulating one's public image.

*Pro bono* work in this context means volunteering your services and talents for a non-profit, charity, social organization, or similar entity. This involvement allows you to work side by side and develop relationships with community (and sometimes regional and national) leaders, such as the general manager of the utility company, chief operating officer of the bank, managing editor of the newspaper, and local television news anchor. You are brought together through a common cause but will have the opportunity to work together rather intimately at times.

*To maximize the effectiveness (TMTE):* Don't volunteer for sole contributor work such as making telephone calls from home or stuffing envelopes. Volunteer for interactive work, where you participate in meetings and serve on committees. Even better, volunteer to chair or lead the toughest committees, such as fund raising, volunteers, or publicity. Take the most highly visible position you can. Still better: Serve in the capacity of calling on local executives for their support, which will guarantee you at least a conversation with your own potential buyers and establish a rudimentary relationship fostered by a third party.

At some point in the process, after working together with high potential people, suggest that you meet or have lunch on your own some time. Sample lead-in: "I've enjoyed working with you over the past three months, and some of the needs you've expressed at the bank are identical to those I've dealt with for several clients. I thought I might be able to give you some ideas, and you might be able to give me some advice."

Last but not least: Choose a cause or event you truly believe in, so that your good works are easily supported, and you are making a difference, not just making contacts.

I've seen people accelerate their acceptance and multiply their prospects through effective and visible pro bono work. Make sure you or the organization sends appropriate press releases to the media. Perfect your quick branding statement, for example, when you're asked what you do after being introduced, state "I'm Mary Moore and I double the productivity of support staffs" or "I'm Ted Carothers and I'm an expert in the acquisition of key talent."

Create a "response statement" that includes your brand and can be delivered within seven seconds. The idea is to quickly convey your brand and then get the other person to talk.

## Commercial Publishing*

By commercial publishing I mean printing articles or books through a third-party, recognizable source, which implicitly serves as a credible sponsor. This can be a magazine, a book publisher, or an association newsletter, to name just a few.[2] You don't have to be paid—although that never hurts—you simply have to be published through someone else's auspices.

Publishing is essential to gravity because your work:

---

[2]Self-publishing is a different story. Self-publishing a book may result in significant revenues, since you don't have to share anything with a publisher, and they may be great for the ego ("I'm an author"). However, they have zero marketing cachet since so many people self-publish so much schlock. We'll talk about Internet and electronic publishing, which is quite valuable in branding, a little further along our gravity wheel.

- Achieves a permanence of sorts
- Can be passed around and shared
- Can be cited in other publications
- Receives a third-party legitimacy
- Allows your name, brand, and ideas to be clearly associated

We'll talk in the following chapter about book publishing as a discrete branding strategy. For now, here are the keys to getting an article published:

1. Find those publications that you determine are read by potential buyers and recommenders of your services.[3]
2. Read several back issues to learn the "voice" or tone of the publication (for example, it prefers interviews, self-tests, graphs, personal experiences, et cetera).
3. Find the editor or managing editor's name on the masthead and write a personal letter of inquiry to that person.
4. Create a one-page letter of inquiry that focuses on what the benefits of the article are to the readers of that publication and not on how good you are. The editor is paid to care about the former, not the latter.
5. Enclose a stamped, self-addressed envelope.

You might receive no response, which is the norm, or you might receive a note that says, "Can't use this idea but try us again in the future," or you might receive permission to submit the article on speculation.

> Commercial publishing may be the single most effective branding device for any consultant. The keys are to think about the reader's needs, write as if you're in a conversation with that single reader, and provide plenty of pragmatic techniques for immediate use.

[3]Three possible sources: (1) *The Guide to Periodic Literature* found in most libraries; (2) *Writer's Market* and *Writer's Digest* (http://writersdigest.com); Writers Digest Books, 9933 Alliance Rd, Cincinnati, OH 45242; (3) visit any mega-bookstore such as Barnes & Noble and peruse the various magazines.

In any article you write, use your brand frequently and early, even in the headline, for example, "The Key to Bullet-Proof Proposals" or "Retention Tips from the Talent Coach."

My advice is to keep at least four letters of inquiry in circulation at all times.[4] When one is rejected, send the same inquiry to a new publication. Keep this up through even two-dozen rejections. (My all-time best seller, *Million Dollar Consulting,* was rejected fifteen times before being accepted by McGraw-Hill, one of the most elite business publishers.) When an article idea is accepted, replace that inquiry with a new one. If you have four in circulation at all times, you will publish consistently.

*TMTE:* Obtain permission to reprint the article (or purchase reprints). Put it in your press kit. Send it in your client mailings. Post it on your website. Use it as a handout when you speak. For its initial six months, send it to prospects as an example of your most recent publishing. Reference it in your interviews. There are few items as leverageable as an article. Turn a series of articles printed in the same source into a formal column appearing monthly, and then syndicate the column to similar publications. (I write a weekly column for the *Providence Business News* called "The Small Business MBA," which is a brand I'm experimenting with and a market I've otherwise not even approached.)

---

A position paper, or "white paper," is simply an article you've written that hasn't been published commercially. It can still fill nearly all of the other branding duties of a published article if you intermingle them.

---

## Position Papers

I often refer to these as "white papers," which has some additional cachet but merely reflects the color of the paper they are printed on (just as automotive

---

[4]There is nothing immoral, illegal, or unethical about sending the same inquiry to different publications, called a "multiple submission." When one accepts, you simply can't publish the same piece with any others.

dealers use "the blue book" for valuations, as if it carries added authenticity, because the book has traditionally had a blue cover).

You should create a minimum of one position paper a quarter. If you have none at all, create one every other month for the next year. These are two-to-six-page *non-promotional* articles that promote your views on issues important to your work and in support of your brand. They may contain charts or graphics but needn't. They must provide real value and practical techniques for the reader.

If you are a technological consultant, a position paper might be entitled "How to Move Knowledge Management to the Front Lines." If you are in the small business market, the paper might be "Instant Valuation for Any Small Business," which also includes a nice brand statement. A succession of such papers on a variety of topics will create a body of work that will help to establish you and your brand as one of the outstanding voices and authorities in your field.

Keep your papers consistent in format and produce them on high quality paper using an excellent printer. A cover page, bibliography, and summary page can all add still more appeal and professionalism. These are easy to do, and you're remiss if you're not creating them regularly.

*TMTE:* Include them in your press kit. Post on your website. Use as handouts when you speak. Use as the basis for interviews. Leave with prospects. Index them and turn them into booklets when you have a sufficient number.

## Radio, Television, and Print Interviews

I'll combine these three elements since they require similar investment and support.

There is a plethora of talk shows on the airwaves and a dearth of intelligent life to appear on them. If you pick and choose your spots, and you're willing to suffer a few minor indignities, radio and TV can reinforce your brand.

There are some excellent sources for ads and listings that are circulated for free to talk show producers, interviewers, assignment editors, reporters, and others in the media. Some of the most effective include:

- *The Yearbook of Experts, Authorities & Spokespersons* (Broadcast Interview Source, 2233 Wisconsin Ave., NW, Washington, DC, 20007, 202/333–4904, www.yearbooknews.com). This book and online listing provides the opportunity to place an advertisement in front of a wide variety of media types, including talk show hosts, producers, assignment editors, reporters, and so on. It also provides other services, such as automated press releases. A half-page ad will probably run from $500 to $750. You can include photos of yourself, book jackets, etc., and be listed in a number of categories for cross-reference (for example, change management, strategy, expert witness, etc.).

- *The Directory of Memberships and News Sources* (The National Press Club of Washington, 529 14th St., NW, Washington, DC, 20045, 202/662–7500, www.npc.press.org). This is similar to the *Yearbook of Experts,* published and distributed by the National Press Club. Costs are roughly the same, although ancillary services are far less.
- *Radio and TV Interview Reporter* (Bradley Communications, 135 E. Plumstead Ave., Lansdowne, PA, 19050, 610/259–1070). An advertising source for radio and television talk shows, published twice a month. They will help you format and design your ad. Cost depends on size and frequency.

> Attack a broadcast media appearance aggressively, with the intent of citing your brand several times. Never rely on the host or the environment to promote you. It doesn't work that way.

On any media appearance, you should *always* prepare yourself with two or three points you will make *regardless of the questions you're asked* and always plan to *prominently mention your brand.* An example: If you're an expert in team building, and the host asks, "What is the reason that there is so little loyalty today toward one's employer?" respond with, "Well, in an article I wrote called 'The Team Builder,' I point out that we really have created committees instead of teams, and no one is loyal to a committee in the workplace." In that one sentence you've mentioned your expertise, an article, and your brand. Don't wait for your spots, *make* your spots.

Occasionally, you'll find yourself on a five-minute, meaningless show with a host who would rather hear his or her own voice than yours; on a call-in show with inane callers; or in a market that's worthless. Don't worry about the lack of impact. You do most radio shows from your home over the phone, and television spots are always going to be pithy due to time constraints.

For print interviews, ask the caller for a sample of the questions. Never agree to be interviewed "on the spot"—always set up a future date when you'll be uninterrupted and prepared. Create those brand identifiers you want to be sure to include, write them down, and work them into multiple responses to the interviewer's questions (because you're never sure what actual questions will be included in the final, edited interview). Spell your name and other pertinent facts at the outset (I've been Alen, Allen, Allan, Alyn, and Lynn; and Wise, Wess, West, Wiess, and Ice).

*TMTE:*

1. Listen to the show several times to understand the host's biases, tone, and approach.
2. Ask the producer in advance about the demographics: who listens and at what times?
3. Prepare one to five points that you will include in your responses *no matter what you are asked.* This is an old political device. In a five-minute interview, one point is all you can manage, but in an hour five points are achievable. (Example: If you're asked about a current company that is in the news for downsizing, your response might include: "Actually, Joan, that's one of the topics that my workshops always address . . ." thereby getting in a plug for your courses.)
4. Ensure that you get a tape. If the station doesn't give one out as a matter of course, offer to provide the blank tape and a mailer. If that is unacceptable, have someone tape the show from the radio on a good piece of equipment (you can't do it yourself unless it's done far from your phone interview or the feedback will bring the roof down).
5. Use notes. When you know the topic in advance, as is usually the case, make some notes about times, dates, examples, and so on so as to appear proficient and knowledgeable. Don't ever try to "wing it."
6. Be prepared for change. The host will sometimes come up with a bright idea at the last minute and ask you to address another topic. Don't get testy. Go with the flow.
7. Use the host's name and speak favorably, for example, "Randy, you just asked a question that I wish I could get corporate America to answer." The more "host friendly" you are, the better chance of a return engagement.

8. Alert people that you'll be on the air. Tell friends, colleagues, clients, prospects, bankers, etc. If you have sufficient lead time, send out a brief press release (email works well here).

9. Ask whether the station will run some promos in advance for your interview spot. You may want to record these if you can find out when they are scheduled.

10. Make copies of the tapes from these collected interviews (for about a dollar apiece) and include them in your press kit, to create tremendous credibility.

11. In print, ask for a copy of the entire publication, not a tear sheet. But also get the date and issue number, because many times you won't be sent one and you'll have to obtain your own. Get reprint permission and place these in your press kit and on your website. Use as a tag line, "as quoted in. . . ."

12. Send your photo to the interviewer, and get the interviewer's address and phone number. A photo sometimes is used to enhance the piece or to fill a "hole"—and if used will require that a substantial portion of your interview be used.

---

Perception is reality. The advertising industry is geared to influence and shape perception. Through effective advertising, you are creating the reality of your brand. Is that worth it? Every time.

## Advertising

Advertising is a good idea if it is *strategic and not tactical*. That is, Apple advertises its brand strategically primarily through television and occasionally print ads to bolster its image, laud its innovation, and take a solid shot at the awkwardness of other operating systems. A retail dealer, however, might advertise, primarily in print, that there will be a special sale next weekend on Apple products, which is a tactical promotion.

Consultants shouldn't be advertising that they're "in town next week" or that their strategy work is at 50 percent during their crazy summer sale days. But they can create gravity for the brand by using well-placed, long-lived, and consistent messages that establish an image and manage perception in their favor.

If a good ad costs $10,000 to run for a year, and you only receive a dozen inquiries, one of which leads to a $95,000 project, you've done quite well; if you receive three hundred inquiries, five of which lead to $20,000, you've done quite poorly. You should strive to create quality, not quantity, in your attraction. Your ad manages perception. Don't allow the perception to be that you're the least expensive alternative or that you'll respond with quotes to low-level inquiries.[5]

Choose your advertising targets with a sole criterion in mind: Who is the reader of the publication? (Broadcast media are not effective advertising alternatives for the profession, because you will almost never be speaking to your potential buyers.) If you advertise in *Training Magazine* or *Training & Development* or *HRMagazine*, your readers are virtually all human resource managers and trainers, with relatively little buying power—and most of that for workshops and off-the-shelf programs. If you advertise in *Harvard Business Review* or *Business Week* or an airline magazine, a good portion of your readers are more likely to be senior managers and executives. If you advertise in *Chemistry Today* or *Insurance News* you'll be reaching a high percentage of senior people in a narrow field.

*TMTE:* Keep an ad in place for an extended period of time. Allow it to whet the appetite (provide outstanding testimonials or an impressive client list) without so much detail that the reader can "deselect" you (you focus on telemarketing for the insurance industry in the northeast). Offer an easy way to contact you (toll-free number, simple email address, alluring website) and offer immediate value (send for our complimentary study of "How to Compensate Top Salespeople." Place the ads in your press kit and use them in letters ("You may have seen our ad in this month's . . .").

## Passive Listings

These are types of ads, perhaps, but are really considered more of a reference source for people seeking various assistance. Some you pay to be a part of;

---

[5]Many consultants in my mentoring program are surprised at demands made by prospects, only to eventually be enlightened that their own advertising and promotion have created those excessive demands and false expectations.

others are free as a service to the profession and/or to those seeking assistance. The most basic passive listing is the local Yellow Pages of the phone book. Quite a few major projects have resulted from someone who was delegated the responsibility of finding "management consultants" or "recruiters" or "compensation specialists" in the local phone book. (In phone books, studies show that people will tend to call those with display ads and those with bold print over those with just regular listings. The psychology seems to be that a more expensive placement indicates a more successful firm.)

Find listings that appeal to your prospective buyers and can support the brand image you're building, and then leave them alone. Don't expect "quick hits" or dramatic results. You're building a brand image, not a short-term sales device.

These passive listings are also excellent sources for interviews, as we've discussed earlier in this chapter.

Listings are often included in "Buyers' Guides" and magazine supplements. They are also quite common on the Internet, again sometimes for free and sometimes at a price. On the basis that none of us is smart enough to know where every high quality lead will originate, it's a good idea to have at least some passive listings working for you. You can place them and forget about them, another nice aspect of "gravity."

*TMTE:* Use bold type or your logo if possible. Use the maximum number of words allowed. Refer people to your web home page. Provide multiple contact points (phone, email, fax). If there's room, put in a testimonial.

The line between consulting and speaking is constantly blurring. You can no longer afford to be a poor presenter. No one is expecting an orator, but you should be able to address a room and hold people's attention. If you can't, get help.

# Speaking*

Standing in front of a room full of buyers and recommenders sponsored by a credible third party is one of the most effective marketing tactics that I know of. Similarly, addressing an in-house meeting where you are instantly introduced to every senior manager and/or key professional is a magnificent opportunity.

You may not choose to become a "professional" speaker, and may not charge for the activity. (I strongly recommend you do, because people believe they get what they pay for and it can become quite a lucrative income stream.[6]) If you think of all those dreadful management meetings you've attended, however, with all those droning executives boring the audience and going well over their time allotments, you can see that a moderately good speaker who follows a few sound rules will appear to be an all-star.

In corporate settings, you're almost bound to look good. In trade association settings, where the convention might have some true professionals on the platform, you'll have to be a little better than moderately good, but not much.

People won't know that you're a speaker unless you inform them, so it must be part of your gravity strategy. Include the fact in your promotional material and website, and use some testimonials specifically about speeches you delivered. Start with simple speeches to local service clubs and civic organizations if you're a neophyte and need to hone your skills and calm your nerves. Speaking coaches are in more abundant supply than mosquitoes in a southern swamp, and a half day with one will usually be sufficient to overcome any serious problems. There are also excellent books on platform techniques and speech preparation.[7]

The key is to be conversational, use notes (never memorize), use anecdotes and real stories from your experiences (so the talk is personalized and uniquely yours), and never be overtly promotional. But always be "softly promotional": Cite examples from your consulting work, name clients, use techniques you learned while engaged in projects, and so forth. Let the audience know that you're a consultant by trade who happens to be speaking to them today.

*Always* make an appointment to meet with the buyer (the vice president of sales, the trade association executive director) *after* the speech, to discuss further relationships and possible projects. Speakers make the mistake of talking *before*

---

[6]See my book *Money Talks: How to Make a Million As a Speaker,* McGraw-Hill, 1998.

[7]*Money Talks* has an annotated bibliography of books on speaking and platform technique.

the speech to prepare, but never after the speech to follow up and build business. Don't make that mistake. For a consultant, speaking is a means to other ends, not an end in and of itself.

Consultants who also speak before groups, and who promote their ability to do so, have far better results in attracting new business than those who do not. One additional benefit: Clients like to minimize, not maximize, consultant use. If you can also speak, then you can present your findings to the management team at a conference or prepare them for the next stage. You can also serve to open or close a conference, meaning less reliance on outside resources.

*TMTE:* Record your talks on audio and/or video, using a professional (sometimes the client will do this for you). Use the tapes as "demo" or audition tapes for other clients and as future product offerings (which we'll discuss later in this chapter). When you're ready, look into bureau representation. They will take about 25 percent of your speaking fee to market you, but it's pay-for-performance only, which is fine. However, don't allow the bureau to take 25 percent of any subsequent consulting work generated by the speech, and make sure that's safeguarded in the contract (a 10 percent courtesy may be appropriate). *Focus primarily on trade associations whose members constitute your potential buyers.*

## Website*

There are many people who know far more about Internet use than I, but you'd never know it by surfing the web. Most sites are ineffective, and most consultant sites are plain lousy.

> Consultants seem to believe that websites are ideal places to explain complex methodologies and to provide biographical sketches. In fact, such "allure" is only sure to drive people back to the search engines.

Here are the criteria for a dynamite website:

- Offers value (articles, techniques, links to other sites, etc.)
- Easily navigable (you can get around easily without going back to the start each time)

- Downloads quickly (assume slower modems for visitors)
- Provides for easy feedback (email to you available for the visitor)
- Aesthetically attractive (use of colors, not endless text)
- Focused on the customer, not on the provider (results that are likely, not methodology and biographical sketches)
- Offers something for sale (offsets costs and can become major passive income)
- Compels the visitor to return and to tell others (monthly changes, controversy, pragmatic techniques, etc.)

No one hops in a car to drive down the highway in order to read billboards and storefront signs. Similarly, people do not surf the web to read ads, intricate methodologies, or biographical sketches. They want to know: *What's in it for me?* Most consultant sites never get around to telling them!

Offer value quickly, provide testimonials and client lists as assurances of quality, create a compelling reason both to return and to tell others, and you have the makings of a great website.

*TMTE:* Find an outstanding web designer, but you write the copy. Consider live audio and/or video (see "Speaking" above), which adds a nice dimension. Don't link to too many other sites, because you want to keep people on your site (I provide no links to anyone or anywhere). Change the site at least quarterly and preferable monthly in some way, even merely through the addition of new articles. Use search engines to cover all your brands, including your name, your company, your specialties, and so forth. If you sign up on a site such as www.submit-it.com, it will list you with all major search engines and update your listing periodically for a modest fee. The site www.namesecure.com will enable you to take any unused name, create email and a site, which are automatically forwarded to you. For example, I've taken AlanWeiss.com, because my name has become a brand, and all email and website inquiries for that domain are automatically forwarded to summitconsulting.com. Finally, a site such as www.spynet.com will keep you apprised of any mentions of whatever brands you register with them anywhere on the Internet. That enables you to locate areas that are talking about you or citing you (that is, the "gravity" is working) so that you can build on it and exploit it.

## Electronic Newsletters

These can be the best of attractions or sure repulsion. There are far more of the latter than the former, so there is a nice opportunity here.

An electronic newsletter should be non-promotional, full of value to the reader, short (one screen, more or less), and easy to read. Therefore:

- Use a large, readable font that you test by sending it to others and asking for feedback from their systems
- Don't use symbols such as curly quotes ("), which tend to translate as strange hieroglyphics on many systems (∞)
- Keep the format absolutely consistent from issue to issue
- Keep the frequency absolutely consistent and on time, whether weekly, monthly, or quarterly
- Use a list server for automated subscriptions, subscription cancellations, and address changes (for example, www.databack.com)
- Always allow the option to "unsubscribe," which is a legal requirement and just plain polite

Some people print out electronic newsletters, but many can't be bothered (or receive them on a laptop on the road) and read them or discard them immediately. Keep these full of value, techniques, and tips, and remember that short, pithy items are better than long narratives. You can write several of these at once so that you have a backlog for use when you travel or are busy with projects.

---

Keep your newsletter brief, ensure that it carries two or three immediately applicable techniques, and include no self-promotion other than your contact information. You want to create brand value, not sales promotion.

Keep your brand apparent, preferably in the title of the newsletter (we started "The Sales Accelerator" for one of my mentor program participants) and often in the text ("I've found that Retain Them or Lose Them works at all levels, according to a recent study conducted by. . . .").

*TMTE:* Place the newsletter subscription information (it should be free to subscribe) in a signature file on all your email. Place it on the first page of your website. Archive the issues on your website, indexed by topic. Place some of them in hard copy in your press kit. In your bio, include that you're publisher of the newsletter. Offer it to clients, or consider a slightly different "client edition." Copyright it.

> Word of mouth is highly effective and can take on a life of its own. Business actually *improves* for most firms that are shown in a negative light on the investigative television show *60 Minutes*.

## Word of Mouth

Word of mouth is often a result of the rest of the gravity tactics working well. A "buzz" is created about you and your brands, and buyers do say, "Get me that Alan Weiss person" or "find the guy they call 'the million dollar consultant.'"

However, you can also stimulate word of mouth on a consistent, cost-effective basis. Here are some ideas to create a "buzz" about yourself and your firm in some likely and unlikely ways not covered or partially covered above:

- Write letters to the editor of national and regional publications, citing your expertise and/or experience in making your point (I've appeared in *Fortune, Frequent Flyer,* and similar publications regularly)
- Volunteer to serve on advisory panels, civic commissions, and task forces
- Have colleagues and acquaintances mention you prominently in return for your doing them the same favor
- Write "op ed" pieces for the local newspaper
- Raise questions from the floor at community meetings, school meetings, shareholder meetings, etc.
- Donate books you've written, articles, and so forth, to libraries, non-profit publications, etc.
- Offer to serve as a judge at a speech or academic competition
- Hand out merchandise or business aids with your name on them
- Serve as an usher, emcee, guide, docent, or in similar positions for public functions
- Contribute financially to charities and fund raisers (*Note:* You will get more attention donating a lot of money to a single cause rather than less money to many causes)

- Determine to be a high bidder for one or more items at a local auction, where the items are likely to be hotly contested
- Take part in a local parade or community event with a float, sponsorship, or other presence
- Sponsor a local sports team

Word of mouth is the epitome of inertia. If it's at rest, it is likely to stay at rest. If it's in motion, it's likely to stay in motion.

*TMTE:* Use a clipping service or other means to track when and where you and your brands are mentioned. Use your business card as a small ad in programs and booster packages. Have them announce from the stage or print in the program that the following performance is made possible by your firm. Ask people whether they've ever heard of your brand, your firm, or your name, and find out why or why not.

## Trade Association Leadership

In for a dime, in for a dollar, the old poker hands would say. You should belong to relevant trade associations, so why not up the ante and your time investment just a bit and offer to be an officer, committee chair, or program head? The chances are that your offer will be synonymous with election/appointment, since most of these associations are starving for qualified leadership.

The visibility from these positions, frankly, has always amazed me. I can connect about $250,000 in business from my serving as president of the New England Speakers Association. While there, I was "dubbed" with a new brand: King of the Speakers, and it stuck. It was worth, literally, a quarter million dollars. Maybe not Midas, but at least princely.

Go for the tough jobs in trade associations, such as fund raising or volunteer coordinator or treasurer. No one wants them, they are high visibility, and you'll be welcomed with open arms.

When serving in these positions, you will tend to be the one providing media quotes, whom new members seek out, whom interested potential customers contact, who is regarded as an avatar of the profession, and who is instantly vested with credibility and excellence. You are always far more credible for having been past president of the Northern California Chapter of the Institute of Management Consultants than for never having heard of the organization.

You're better off with leadership in just a couple of higher profile trade associations than membership in dozens. Pick and choose those that interest you, can use your help, and that can add to your gravity.

*TMTE:* Choose the toughest, ugliest, least successful jobs (treasurer, program chair, membership director) and apply yourself. You'll shine as the person who turned around the worst situation (which are, ironically, always the easiest to turn around). Use the position as an opportunity to network and learn about the market and competitive activity. Earn an award or two ("Member of the Year," "Symbol of the Profession"), which you can cite in your literature, on your website, etc.

---

Referrals are simply the most important aspect of branding and marketing. More consultants are leaving more money on the table by ignoring this "gravitational pull" than for any other reason.

## Third-Party Referrals, Endorsements, Testimonials*

I've included these as one category because they are so closely related and synergistic.

When I was first married in the late 60s, a Prudential insurance agent called on me and, because I worked at the company, sold me a small policy. His name was Hal Mapes. I still remember, because Hal had an incredible sales technique: He would visit me twice a year to explore my insurance needs and, regardless of my needs or lack of them, *always* asked me for three names he could call on. When I said, "Gee, Hal, I don't know anyone else who would be interested," he replied, "That's okay, take your time, I can wait." I realized that he wasn't leaving until I came up with three names.

After a while, I would prepare the names well in advance of Hal's visit in order to get him out of the house! Hal retired a wealthy guy. Did all the leads pay off? Of course not. But enough of them did, and then they provided leads who provided still more leads. . . .

Educate your clients early. Tell them that you'll be asking them for referrals, testimonials, and references once the project is successful (*not* after it's over and you've left). Ask them repeatedly. There is nothing as golden as a buyer telling a peer, "You need Alan Weiss for your project." The next best technique is to say, "I know you're familiar with Harriet Stone, and she's provided this wonderful endorsement of my work."

Most consultants—even veteran, successful ones—do not mine this rich source of relatively easy business acquisition. Brand endorsement is extraordinarily powerful (which is why so many commercials and advertisements use well-known endorsers), so capitalize on this fact continually.

For the record: A *testimonial* is a letter, paragraph, or other promotion in writing extolling your ability; a *reference* is someone who agrees to be contacted by your prospects; and a *referral* is a name from a current client to someone who may become a client. There is no reason on earth why you can't solicit all three from a delighted, current client.

*TMTE:* Create a testimonial book devoted to the purpose. Also, create full pages crammed with references. The result is that prospects are so overwhelmed that they seldom call anyone, thereby shortening the sales process. Include testimonials and references on your website and on all your printed material. Send a token of appreciation to anyone providing a referral, *irrespective of whether or not it results in business.* Try to have your brand(s) included in every testimonial.

## Print Newsletters

We've become a newsletter society, and a print newsletter is ideal for conveying your image and brand. (Electronic newsletters can seldom accurately and reliably convey logos and colors and certain formats.)

Print newsletters should be non-promotional, four color, and consistent in frequency and distribution. Quarterly is minimal, bi-monthly probably optimal. Don't even include client testimonials; focus solely on providing quality and value associated with your brand. Include contact information, and it's OK to sell a product or two if you have them (see later in this chapter).

Some people charge for print newsletters. This can be highly successful, in that the costs are defrayed and profit is even possible (one of mine was bought out by an alliance partner and I became a paid editor of the new incantation). People do believe they get what they pay for.

Use four-color, four pages, no self-promotion, and unyielding publication dates for consistency. If you can't fill it yourself, invite "guest" authors to contribute, but make sure the quality is top-rate.

But don't forget that the primary purpose is brand promotion and marketing gravity. You're not in the newsletter business, you're in the consulting business, and newsletters are a means to that end. However, they can establish you as an authority in your field since you control the content, and they can establish your brand as the *ne plus ultra*.

*TMTE:* Consider guest articles and columns to take the strain off yourself and offer still more value. Include subscription information in your email signature file. Post some of the articles on your website, along with subscription information. Include inserts that promote your products and services. Enter it

# VIGNETTE

I started *The Consultant's Craft* several years ago, a bi-monthly for consultants. My intent was to build that brand as synonymous with myself and practical advice for practice management.

A potential alliance partner approached me and offered a series of very positive joint ventures, but demanded that part of our deal be that I sell them the newsletter, which was remodeled into a monthly called *What's Working in Consulting,* which I now edit. They saw my newsletter as too much potential competition for their own similar publications.

At the time of the sale, my subscription list was only about three hundred people! Yet the growing brand and its impact in the market was enough to represent a very valuable asset for me. Brand potential can be as important as brand existence.

In the newsletter business, you never know just how much you may be able to increase your base.

in a newsletter competition, so that any honor won can enable you to cite it as the "award winning newsletter."

> Interviews should be controlled by the interviewee, not the interviewer. That sounds counter-intuitive, but it's the only effective marketing technique you can apply. You have one shot—it must be your ammunition.

## Teaching

College and professional school enrollments are surging, and good schools like to augment their faculties with pragmatic, "real world" practitioners. If you approach universities, colleges, junior colleges, trade schools, university extension programs, and similar institutions, the probability is that you can find a part-time teaching job that suits your schedule.

I've taught in the Graduate School of Business at the University of Rhode Island for four years, one night a week, to MBA and Ph.D. candidates. I've been a visiting professor or lecturer at Case Western Reserve (for seven years), the University of Illinois, St. John's, the Graduate School of Business at the University of Georgia, Johnson & Wales (a culinary and hotel management school), New England Tech (a trade school), and the Institute of Management Studies, among others. Former students have approached me for bids on projects at their businesses (most of my students are adults studying at night). I'm able to list in my biographical sketch that I hold an adjunct professor's appointment.

> Teaching provides credibility for all of your branding "gravity" elements. Work your brand into the mix. I also assign one or two of my books in my own classes, and the students love it.

At Case Western Reserve and at the Institute of Management Studies, the institutions would assemble large groups of executives for me to address at scheduled times throughout the year (the latter in Europe as well as the U.S.). Any ensuing business from those sessions was strictly mine.

Teaching adds credibility to your brand, enables you to "pay back" for your success, and also provides a pragmatic view of what people are facing on their jobs at the moment in non-client and diverse companies. The institutions usually will at least partially publicize your appointment and your courses, sometimes aggressively so. You will also meet people who can recommend you to others who are buyers in their organizations. (And, not insignificantly, some of these institutions pay you to do this. It's not a king's ransom but it will pay for vacations and mortgages. I use my university income to support my hobbies.)

*TMTE:* Send press releases out about your appointment. If you have a book, use it as one of your course books. Use your brand in the course description material. Set up major organizational projects for your students with local top executives, which is a fine reason to establish a relationship with them. Offer to serve on school committees, and/or to provide *pro bono* services for the faculty and administration (as a facilitator, strategist, etc.).

## Alliances*

As a solo practitioner or a small firm owner (or even as a practice managing partner in a large firm), one of the great leverage elements for your brand is in a synergistic alliance with someone who perceives a win/win potential *and who offers a marketing advantage that you do not possess.*

> The equation in any alliance is 1 + 1 = 64. That is, there must be exponential growth for both parties far above the costs of managing the alliance. Two parties making a million dollars each combining to make $2.5 million are actually losing ground.

*Example:* I have an alliance with Kennedy Information, which publishes a host of newsletters and books, including *Consultant's News.* They can market to more people, more quickly, and more cost effectively than I ever could. I can provide them with consulting expertise, writing ability, and presentation skills that would be hard to combine and very expensive to obtain otherwise. So, Kennedy promotes high-end consulting seminars, which I deliver, they publish my most expensive specialized books on subjects such as proposal writing, and I edit their newsletter for solo practitioners.[8] We each profit handsomely and reach audiences we might not otherwise be able to reach.

Find alliance partners whose own brands do not conflict with yours. Some guidelines beyond that:

- You must trust them implicitly. No contract can ever protect you adequately. This must be based on strong chemistry and confidence in the other party.
- Use simple formulas, such as splitting profits 50/50 after all costs.
- Establish clear payment guidelines, for example, within ten days of any event, once per quarter.
- Do not stint on mutual promotion. You have an accountability to your partner.
- Create a methodology to work together that is least time demanding for you. Work your accountabilities into your schedule. Many otherwise fine alliances fail because deadlines are missed or an inordinate amount of work is perceived to be required, distracting one party from more mainstream activities.
- Constantly search for ways to expand the alliance content. These are organic relationships that should be nurtured and grown, not left on a plateau. Along those lines, meet personally with your partners at least once a quarter to guarantee that you remain on their "radar screen." The larger the partner, the more important this is.
- Form several alliances and don't become overly dependent on any one. Don't allow any partner to constitute even a quarter of your revenues, or you're not very independent any more (just as no client should be so overwhelming). *Rule of thumb:* You should be able to lose any single client or any single alliance partner and not suffer a major threat to your life style or business plans.

---

[8]*What's Working in Consulting.* Write or email me for a free copy.

*TMTE:* Seek out alliance partners who have maximum distribution potential, preferably global. If you have products, place them into that network, even at a discount. Get early agreement for your brand, logo, tag line, contact information, or whatever, to accompany all descriptive material, promotional literature, and so on. Create mutual web links. Make absolutely sure you copyright and trademark that which is your proprietary intellectual property, so that you avoid blurring of those important lines of demarcation.

## Products

I have become a huge advocate of creating products early—and creating plenty of them. These include manuals, checklists, booklets, pamphlets, books (both commercially published and self-published), audiotapes, videotapes, CDs, newsletters, and other related materials.[9]

Products can and will do the following:

- Promote your brand in the titles and content
- Create a revenue stream
- Add value to your press kit
- Provide "leave behinds" and handouts
- Add to your credibility
- Serve as transient marketing elements that are passed around
- Differentiate you from the competition
- Allow you to avoid RFPs and become a "sole source" provider[10]

Create products at first by combining position papers, articles, and interviews into booklets, and then booklets into books. Use audio- or videotape at a speech, hire a professional editor, and create a product on your special brand.

---

[9]And I am rabidly against bumper stickers, coffee mugs, T-shirts, and other irrelevant stuff that simply confuses whether you're a consulting firm or a flea market.

[10]One of the banes of consulting is the government Request for Proposal, which demands an expensive and laborious response, which government buyers then use to determine who is cheapest and, generally, apply all the wrong criteria to. By publishing a book, you can become a "sole source" provider not subject to competitive bidding, because you are the sole source of that book and its content and a government buyer can specifically request you as a resource.

People buy print first, audio second, and video third. Whenever appropriate, combine them and the power of the first will improve the sale of the latter two.

Ultimately, you should write a book about each of your brands, and we'll cover this in the next chapter. There is absolutely nothing like a commercially published book for credibility and brand recognition (just think of *The One Minute Manager* or *The Learning Organization*).

*TMTE:* Create a product catalog, both in print and on your website. Solicit testimonials from the sources and in the manner mentioned earlier in this chapter. Include product inserts with your mailing. Provide a blurb about your newest product in your email signature file. Obtain an ISBN (International Standard Book Number) for your books and tapes, and have them listed on Amazon.com and other Internet distribution sources. Ask your alliance partners to carry the products amidst their own offerings. *Always* offer your clients your products at a courtesy discount, and always send a free copy to your buyer.

Networking is about quality, not quantity. Most people who think they are "networking" are actually wasting their time and everyone else's, and they might as well be home with a good book—probably this one.

## Networking

We've now come "full circle" on our gravity field to the old standby, networking. Let's make one thing clear from the outset: Networking is about *giving, not receiving.* Networking is interactive pursuit of others and development of reciprocally beneficial relationships and brand identification through interpersonal, telephonic, electronic, and correspondence activities.

Among those who constitute networking potential for your brands are:

- buyers
- media people
- key vendors
- mentors
- endorsers
- meeting planners

- recommenders to buyers
- bankers
- key advisors
- high profile individuals in your business
- trade association executives
- community leaders

Here's how you network above and beyond the commonplace: Here is a sequence for networking, whether at a trade association meeting, civic event, business conference, recreational outing, or nearly any other activity you know in advance you'll be attending:

1. Learn who will likely attend the event. Obtain a participant list, a brochure, the names of the committee members—or make an educated guess.
2. Begin casual conversations during the gathering, both to identify those targets you've chosen and to learn who else might be there who could be of help.
3. Introduce yourself without describing anything about your work and simply listen to them. If in a group, which is likely, don't attempt your personal networking. *Wait until you can find the person alone later, and approach him or her one-on-one, preferably where you will have a few minutes in private.*
4. When you're able to spend a few minutes one-on-one, offer something of value, based on what you've heard. For example, if the person is a potential buyer who has mentioned the problem she's having with attracting and retaining good people, suggest a book that you would be happy to pass along or a website that you'll send by email that has articles on the subject.
5. In the event you're asked what you do, practice providing very succinct responses: "I assist clients in improving individual and organizational performance." (If the other person says, "That's a bit vague. How do you do that?" then you reply, "Well, if you tell me something about your organization and the issues you're facing, I'll show you how the approaches may apply specifically to you.")
6. Exchange cards or somehow gather the other person's contact information

so that you can send the promised material or information. At a minimum get a phone number and email address.

7. Immediately, the next morning at the latest, deliver what you promised. If you're providing the other party as a resource to someone else, then copy that person on the email or correspondence, or mention to the person that you've given his or her name to the individuals you had mentioned.

8. In a week or so, follow up to see whether the material was helpful, the reference worked out, the prospects called, etc. Ask if there is anything further along those lines that might be helpful. Then, summarize or reaffirm your offer of further help with a letter accompanied by your promotional material and literature.

---

Networking should be focused and targeted, a series of "rifle shots," not an amorphous blob overrunning a meeting or wild shotgun fire. Pick your targets of opportunity carefully, and develop them.

---

9. In a few weeks, send still more value in the form of a contact, potential customer, article of interest, etc.

If the other party replies with a "thank you" for your latest offer of value, then get back to the person and suggest a brief meeting, breakfast, lunch, or other opportunity to get together at his or her convenience. Simply say that you'd like to learn more about what the person does and also get his or her advice about what you do. If the person has not responded with a "thank you" of any kind, then wait one more week, call to see whether the person received the additional value you sent, and then suggest the meeting as described above. (An active response simply enables you to shorten the waiting time.)

*TMTE:* Provide some insights into the other person's work through some careful homework. Listen more than you talk. Always try to get people one-on-one, away from the crowd. If you promise anything, do it the next morning. Add all key people to your mail lists. Have the host or some important third party provide a personal introduction to your highest priority targets. Have a colleague or friend mention you to those targets in their own casual conversations as someone they should definitely meet.

## BRAND NEW LESSONS

Your gravitational field can be as large or as small as you choose. Once established, elements should remain in place, because you never know which element will attract which type of potential client. Ensure that your brands are integrated into your marketing elements.

The gravity alternatives are clearly interrelated and overlap. Exploit that duplication and leveraging, so that a single exertion on your part creates multiple allure. As you grow in this business, your gravity field should grow commensurately. All of the elements I've explained I have constantly in place, promoting quite a few differing brands.

What are you doing to attract buyers to you?

# CHAPTER 4

# How to Write a Book, Even If You've Never Written Your Mother

## *The Best Branding Technique of Them All*

There is probably no better branding technique than a published book. That's because a commercially published book provides these immediate benefits:

- An implicit third-party endorsement (the publisher)
- Significant distribution through stores and the Internet
- Availability through your own devices (website, catalog, etc.)
- Word of mouth
- Copyright
- Reviews and excerpts in circulation
- Book club representation

- Credibility by dint of the feat itself
- Possible translation into other languages
- Possible alteration for audio, video, seminars, and so forth
- Eventual publishing in paperback
- Enhanced desirability as a speaker
- Greater ability to publish articles based on the book
- Interview opportunities in all media
- Readership, ranging from modest numbers to many thousands

It's important to note that I speak of a "commercially published book," that is, one from an acknowledged major publisher (for example, Jossey-Bass/Pfeiffer, John Wiley & Sons, McGraw-Hill, and so on). Self-published books, on the other hand, can serve to provide revenue streams (because the author/publisher keeps most of the revenues and not just the royalties), but simply do not have the cachet or credibility of commercial publishing. Potential buyers are not stupid, and they can recognize a vanity piece, no matter how well written, at a hundred yards.

So, the key is to attract a major publisher. I'm going to address that effort below, and cover early preparation, the treatment or proposal, the actual writing, and the marketing effort.

A book will establish you as a unique resource and brand (if you choose your topic and approach correctly) and can even make you a "sole source" provider for government agencies and private firms that use RFPs (requests for proposals), eliminating the tedious, unprofitable, and usually unsuccessful requirements for competitive bidding.

A word of caution. It is easier and more productive to publish a book than ever before, thanks to computers, a global marketplace, and an increasingly educated public's thirst for learning. However, therein is also the rub: Few books last for more than a brief wink in the morning sun, and a single major publisher might launch thousands of books a year with the hope that some will gain favor on the basis of virtually no marketing support. As in all things, publishers bank on the big names, who don't need the support, and give short shrift to newcomers, who desperately need it—not unlike banks and their lending policies.

Having said that, these rapids can be navigated, and I'd like to help you to understand the necessary charts and hazards. *Note:* I'm going to reduce writing a book to an orderly, systematic exercise. You may feel free to depart from my structure at any time and let the creative juices flow. But I want to establish a fail-safe approach to getting a book in print, particularly for those who never imagined they could do so.

> Publishing is an ironic pursuit, in which you need the assistance of heavyweight publishers and, after acquiring it, must largely fend for yourself.

## EARLY PREPARATION IS BETTER THAN THE BEST EDITOR

Your initial preparation is simple, but vital: Choose a theme for the book (which can become the working title, since the publisher will reserve the right to change the title and generally does so) that is original and unique. Don't write the 50,000th book on why teamwork is important; write the first book that describes why it's overdone and over-hyped and why committee systems are better than teams. Don't create a work that extols customer service, but rather one that describes why the customer is *not* always right.

Remember this above all: Your initial buyer is not the reader, but the acquisitions editor or a literary agent (we'll talk about the pros and cons of approaching each below). Your initial sale, therefore, is to a person who is somewhat jaded, has seen it all, and is looking for something—particularly from an untried author—that will stand out in a crowd. There is no need to be outrageous, but there is a need to be original—and bold. A book proposal must pass the "So what?" test with a tough customer.

Here are the two early preparation steps:

### 1. Choose a Theme

Choose a theme that represents these components:

- There is an existing market appeal or potential appeal you can create
- You have competency and credentials in the area

- You have experiences that allow you to provide examples
- You have a passion for the topic
- The field is not too crowded
- The topic is enduring, not a fad or current "hot issue"

Try to think a year ahead, because that's about the time a successful book will go from early preparation to the bookshelves. Don't spend a lot of time on cute titles or memorable wording. That can all be changed in due course, and the theme itself is far more important, since many great mottoes don't rate a book.

Let's assume for our purposes that we've chosen the following theme: The Customer Isn't Always Right: Finding and Retaining Great Customers, and Letting Go of All the Rest (hereafter referred to as "Customer").

## 2. Create a Table of Contents

The next step is to give substance to your theme, while also preparing for the proposal that lies ahead. The ideal way to do this, and to organize your later writing efforts, is to create a table of contents right away.

Bear in mind that a hardcover book—and you want to commercially publish in hard cover if at all possible to maximize the advantages detailed at the beginning of this chapter—requires a minimum of about 200 book pages, which is the equivalent of 250 to 300 manuscript pages. Therefore, you need to prepare for that length intelligently at the outset, and the table of contents is where to do it.

Write down, as a laundry list, the major elements that support your theme. Don't pay attention to priority or sequence, just write them down. Try to create at least fifteen or twenty. For our Customer theme, here's a sample:

- The types of customers
- The best customers
- The worst customers
- Employee interactions
- Handling difficult situations
- Repeat customers
- Word of mouth
- Retaining customer loyalty
- Legitimate complaints

- Customer feedback
- Maximizing average sales amount
- Involving customers in business decisions
- How to get rid of undesirable customers
- Mail, phone, Internet, and in-store customers and distinctions
- The history of customers
- Shopping your own business as a customer

Note that the words aren't pretty, and there are probably duplications ("worst customers" and "handling difficult situations") as well as minor points that don't deserve a whole chapter ("the history of customers"). Nonetheless, I've created my list, and now I can assemble my table of contents.

> One buyer at a time: Focus on the acquisitions editor and/or agent first, because they have to buy your book before any reader even gets close to it.

Now, let's assume you'll create a 250-page book of ten chapters of twenty-five pages each. It might not eventually work out so evenly, but you have to begin somewhere, and this is as good a method as any. (More chapters make for easier reading than fewer, longer chapters.) This means we'll have to select ten of our laundry list items and make them chapters in some degree of intelligent sequence. *All of this can always be changed later, but you have to start somewhere.* I've seen hundreds of wishful but unpublished authors spend their valuable time trying to choose the perfect title, ideal number of chapters, and absolutely correct wording, with the result that they never write so much as an introduction.

My example will involve the following from our list above:

Chapter 1: The types of customers and their buying habits
Chapter 2: The customers you want to keep, and the customers you want to kill
Chapter 3: Moments of truth: employee/customer interactions
Chapter 4: How to build customer loyalty every single day
Chapter 5: How to handle difficult situations with positive outcomes

Chapter 6: Avoiding bad customers and getting rid of rotten apples
Chapter 7: The impact of the Internet
Chapter 8: Improving per-sale amounts with no investment
Chapter 9: Involving customers in their own retention
Chapter 10: Shopping your own business as your own toughest customer

I've added some pizzazz, used a sequence that I find methodical, and incorporated actions and "how to's" so that the book does not appear to be theoretical, but rather a practical guide that can be used immediately. Remember that none of this is yet etched in granite, and switching Chapters 5 and 6 will have no impact on the outcome of western civilization. The trick is to simply, at this stage, get on with it!

As a final part of your initial work and bridge to the next step, create a manila folder with a label representing each of the chapters. As you read something, hear of something and make a note, or print something from the Internet, place it in the appropriate folder. At the end of a month, if a folder is empty or

## VIGNETTE

My first book, *The Innovation Formula,* was written with a co-author, Mike Robert. In our blissful ignorance—neither of us had published before—we completed the manuscript and sent it to eighteen publishers who, in our one hour of research at a bookstore, seemed to publish similar business books.

Then we sat back.

Within a month, we received five inquiries, which led to three offers. We accepted the one we thought was best for us after personally visiting the three publishers.

This was not the best way to do it, but it somehow worked. My point is that sometimes it's better to be lucky than good. Anything you read here is intended to provide you with the best possible odds of success in publishing. But there will always be exceptions.

That, however, was the first and only time I wrote a complete book before having a proposal accepted. No sense pushing my luck. . . .

How to Establish a Unique Brand in the Consulting Profession

sparsely populated, you've either chosen a poor topic, or you haven't been reading/researching widely enough.

Now that your initial work is done, you're ready to create a proposal.

## CREATING AND SELLING A BRILLIANT PROPOSAL

The agent or acquisitions editor will not want to see a completed manuscript, and you shouldn't put in that much work without a deal from someone. Most nascent authors make the mistake of doing too much writing at the beginning and not enough planning.

The next step is to create a book proposal, or what I usually call a "treatment." Before I begin on that approach, let me briefly clarify the pros and cons of using a literary agent.

Agents can be wonderfully helpful, *if they are good agents.* Unfortunately, not all are, so put careful work into this selection process if you go this route.

### Pros of an Agent

An agent (or at least a good one) has access to acquisitions editors, and the latter will almost always review proposals put forward by agents they trust and respect. The agent will tell you immediately whether your proposal and book theme are up to snuff and whether further work needs to be done prior to approaching editors. An agent will also negotiate the best possible contract, including advance amounts, royalty increase points, free books, free indexing, foreign rights, and other arcana created by legions of lawyers and to be found in every publisher's contract. Agents know what's needed in the market, and also know which publishers are in the market for what types of books.

### Cons of an Agent

You will surrender about 15 percent of everything you earn to the agent, who will receive the publisher's check and forward you your money after commissions are deducted. Agents represent a lot of authors, so you may not receive a strong focus, particularly if other projects are potentially more lucrative than yours. Some agents are glacier-like slow in responding to you. Once you're involved with an agent, you can't easily go to another (with the same project) and you have to pay commissions even if you are independently approached or you sell the book to a publisher yourself through other means.

Having said all that, and having sold books directly to acquisitions editors and through agents, I'd recommend that a new author always attempt to utilize a good agent. How to find a good agent? The same way you find a good client: Network, ask for recommendations, have someone make introductions, stop by in person, and so on. Develop a relationship no less than you would with a high-potential client. Finally, make sure the chemistry is right and that you trust the person implicitly.

## Checklist: Creating a Great Proposal

Here are the steps for your proposal. You can accomplish these in any order that pleases you.

*1. Sample Chapter.* Write a single chapter from the book of the requisite twenty-five pages. It does not have to be the first chapter. Choose one you feel particularly strongly about, or for which your manila folder has the most interesting material. (See the section below on writing the book for advice on how to actually write the chapter if you need help.) Double space the writing and include subheads ("Creating a Great Proposal" above is an example of a subhead), as well as any interviews, charts, graphs, tests, or other features that would naturally appear in the book.

*2. Introduction.* Write the introduction to the book. This should be no longer than two pages and should contain the reason (as expressed to the reader) for the book's creation, what the reader can expect to learn, and how best to approach the book.

*3. Chapter Summaries.* Include the table of contents you've already created, but include one or two paragraphs about each of the chapters (except the one you're writing in full).

*Example:* Moments of Truth: Employee Customer Interactions. This chapter deals with the little-appreciated fact that the lowest paid employees have the most impact on the customer: receptionists, secretaries, repair people, and others. It's imperative that they be trained, motivated, and rewarded for the "moments of truth" that can never be reclaimed. During relatively brief intervals, a customer feels that the value is worth almost any price, or that the poor service doesn't justify coming back again. This chapter will provide techniques to identify and maximize the thousands of "moments of truth" occurring every day.

**4. *Specify Your Audiences.*** Discuss your primary, secondary, and tertiary audiences. Let the editor know for whom this book is intended, and what they will receive from the experience.

*Example:* Primary audience: Business owners and top level executives who wish to increase sales, profitability, and performance. They will learn how to allocate their resources to ensure that the best customers receive the best service, and that the worst customers are not retained.

Secondary audience: Mid- and front-line managers who supervise personnel dealing with the customer. They will be able to establish priorities and base their decisions on profit, not the volume of complaints or the frequency of low-profit transactions.

Tertiary audience: Front-line personnel dealing with customers daily. They will learn that the customer isn't always right and that corporate profitability is determined by their actions, which should not be submissive to any customer demand, no matter how outrageous.

---

In establishing your proposal, you should also invigorate yourself for the writing that will eventually follow. If you don't, then your topic is probably driven by what you think you ought to do, rather than by what you should do.

**5. Evaluate the Competition.**   Do the necessary market research. Go to a large bookstore (or order from the Internet, but visiting the bookstore is easier and less expensive) and pull all the books on related topics from the shelves. Analyze their strengths, and determine why and how yours will be better and stronger, or more unique. (In this exercise, you'll also discover which publishers are marketing books on your topic, meaning that you'll know whom to approach should you decide not to use an agent.) In your proposal, cite these books and, without bad-mouthing them, demonstrate why yours is better, fills an unfilled niche, has unique features, etc.

*Never* tell an agent or editor that there are no competing books, or you will be dismissed out of hand, since there is nothing new under the sun. There are *always* competing books, which means there is a good market for yours. Try to include at least six competing works to demonstrate that you've done your homework and to give the editor some basis of comparison.

**6. Blow Your Own Horn.**   Establish why you are the right person to write this book. Explain your credentials, background, experiences, clients, and so forth. Demonstrate that you bring a unique perspective and view. Cite any articles or interviews you've done (or, of course, any other books). Make a strong case for your *brand.*

**7. Identify the Unique Marketing Edge.**   Detail a uniqueness of the book. For example, some books have interviews with people knowledgeable in the field or with customers; some have self-tests and checklists; others have extensive charts and graphs. Provide any insights into how the work may convey unique market advantages.

**8. Mark Your Promotional Stake.**   Explain how you will contribute to the marketing. Publishers love to know that their initial press run is protected.[1] Do you speak before audiences who will purchase your book in the back of the room? Do you have a website that will sell the book? Do you have a mailing list of sev-

---

[1]Believe it or not, most business books have only an initial press run of a few thousand, if that. About five thousand sales will pay for the book's total costs, and 7,500 will show a profit. At 15,000 or 20,000 in sales, the publisher and/or editor will be saying, "Let's do lunch!"

eral thousand highly qualified clients and potential purchasers? Are there major clients who might buy the book in volume? Provide any mouth-watering marketing help that will whet the publishing appetite.

Your overall treatment, depending on the size of the sample chapter you submit, will run from forty to sixty pages. This is the professional proposal that will gain you an agent or interest an acquisitions editor.[2]

If you use an agent, trust your fate to the agent's hands. If you pursue acquisitions editors directly, find the publishers who are producing books like yours (remember the market research phase above) and call their switchboards to find out the names of the acquisitions editors for business books. Then write to them by name with a cover letter, enclosing your treatment. A simultaneous email wouldn't hurt. Better yet: Find out whether you can network sufficiently to find a third-party introduction or even endorsement. (You might find that the publisher has produced a book by an acquaintance of yours who wouldn't mind making an introduction.)[3]

## WRITING A BOOK AND LIVING TO TELL ABOUT IT

Once you've secured the contract, you can begin to write the book, which means the first step is scheduling, not writing.

*1. Plan.* Take out a calendar and work backwards from your due date for manuscript completion. Most publishers will provide at least six months. Eliminate the final month all together (to be used only in case of emergency) and assume you have five months, starting today. That means you have to write two chapters a month, one every two weeks, which is a piece of cake.

---

[2]For details on proposals, you can access Jeff Herman's many fine books on the subject by searching under his name on Amazon.com. Also, publishers' websites will often contain guidelines and parameters. This book's publisher, Jossey-Bass/Pfeiffer, for example, does a very good job of it.

[3]If you use the direct route and are offered a contract, have your lawyer look it over before the publisher owns rights to your children and your Mercedes.

Determine when you prefer to write. I prefer to write early in the morning, unmolested, so I block out time from about 7 a.m. to 9 a.m. Two hours is my limit, and I can write ten pages—half a chapter—in two hours. That means that two such sessions will produce a chapter. So, for me, four two-hour sessions during a month will produce the requisite two chapters for that month.

Your times and durations may be different. For neophytes, before you are familiar with your actual, reasonable output, I suggest that you assign a morning, from about 8 to noon (or an afternoon, if you prefer, from 1 to 5) for your writing. Forward your phone and/or go somewhere with your computer where you will be undisturbed. The first key is: Schedule reasonable blocks of time to write one chapter every two weeks.

Writing a book is no less a project than implementing changes within a client. You must schedule the time, prepare for the encounter, and remain flexible at all times.

*2. Plan Again, for Contingencies.*   Next, plan *contingency time frames,* so that you have fall-back positions if your original scheduled times should be usurped by client demands or family crises (playing with the dog or washing the car is not a family crisis in this definition). If you've planned to write on a Thursday, perhaps Saturday will be your contingency if Thursday is needed elsewhere. If you make no such official contingencies, you will fall behind very early on, *and there is nothing worse in writing a book than falling behind in your plan.* Thus, the second key is contingency planning.

*3. Write.*   When you write, if you have writer's block or are simply uncertain how to proceed, use this simple formula:

- For every chapter, list five key points. These will become your subheads. For example, in our first chapter, "The Types of Customers and Their Buying Habits," our five points might be:

The browser
The impulse buyer
The loyalist

The comparison shopper
The "cost is no object" shopper

- Each subhead should generate about five pages, thus creating a twenty-five-page chapter.
- Support each subhead with a page each of anecdotes, examples, statistics, narrative, interviews, case studies, and so forth. Take your pick, or choose fewer at two pages each. Hence, for the browser subhead, you may include:

Your own experience as an inveterate browser
How to recognize a browser
What managers have told you about browsers
Examples of browser habits
Statistics about how many people entering a store actually buy

Before you know it, you have a subhead completed, then several, then the chapter. Use your manila folder system to provide content for the subheads, and organize your points to create a logical flow.

However, the third key is this: Writing is about success, not perfection, and we're not talking about *The Grapes of Wrath* or *Atlas Shrugged* here. Besides, the publisher will have both development editors and copy editors who will recommend tightening, elimination of dull stretches, recombination of points, and so forth. Your job, for now, is to create a readable, decent manuscript, not The Great American Novel.

My simple formula will get you through the tough stretches. There will also be times when your manila folder is chock-full, your passion is on the rise, and you wax eloquent for ten pages on a subhead or thirty-five pages for a chapter. That's all fine and well. I'm only trying to kick start the process, and you should feel free to deviate from it toward greater output.

But this point remains: Anyone with discipline, commitment, and basic writing skills can create a book well inside of six months. Anyone who possesses those attributes in great richness can do so in three months. I can, if pressed, write a book in five days (four hours to a chapter, ten chapters require forty hours, divided by an eight-hour day, equals five days), although I prefer to take several months because I write much better at leisure.

Finally, make sure that you often re-emphasize your brand throughout the book, whether it be your name, your program, your approach, your accolades, or whatever. Example: "This concept of finding the true buyer and building a relationship before attempting to close a sale is the essence of what I call 'million dollar consulting,' which I've been practicing and teaching for over a decade."

> A business book has to be good, not great. In fact, Peter Drucker is the only person who has written great business books, so there's no need to feel guilty about creating a merely good one.

Using this system, you can create your book without undue stress or time. You will receive commentary from the development editor asking for backup or rewrites as required, but you have the option to contend these. However, I've seldom worked with an editor who did not improve my books, so leave your ego at home and try to comply with all reasonable requests.

## MARKETING YOUR BOOK BECAUSE THE PUBLISHER REALLY WON'T

Publishers will provide questionnaires and contact points and all kinds of promising marketing goodies, but in the end, you're left to your own devices. With the exception of celebrity books, which the publisher will shamelessly flaunt and flog, all other books are left to their own survival tactics, not unlike the large batch of eggs laid by huge sea turtles. Although millions hatch, only a scant handful avoid predators and grow to their potential. The same with books, particularly first books from any author.

Mark my words, if you're going to publish a book, be prepared to market it and regard anything the publisher does as gravy, and not the other way around. If you're lucky, the publisher will come up with some book clubs and maybe foreign rights (my books have been translated into German, Italian, and Chinese), but that's about it. (Ironically, the publisher will tout the book if your own efforts produce promising sales, which is like a bank offering a loan after it learns you've hit the lottery.)

### Checklist: The Ultimate Marketeer

Here are some marketing guidelines that must go hand in hand with your book effort:

1. Create a budget. Plan on spending your own money to support your book. If you're reading this series, you're a successful consultant, so allot some of your positive cash flow specifically to book marketing.
2. Create an account with a book wholesaler, such as Ingram. You can buy your books at a 40 percent or better discount, earn another 2 percent by paying within ten days, *and* gain royalties from the publisher since the wholesaler must buy from the publisher. The result is a better deal than you get with your straight author's discount from the publisher.
3. Send a book with a cover letter to every reviewer, newsletter editor, magazine, and newspaper that is appropriate. Keep your cover letter to one page, but use parts of your treatment as your argument (what's in it for the reader). As you receive reviews, clip them to your cover letter to still other reviewers.
4. Take listings in the sources mentioned earlier in terms of marketing gravity for media interviews. Use a photo of the book and include any reviewer's favorable commentary.
5. Send free samples to all your major buyers, and offer volume discounts.
6. Ensure that Amazon.com and other Internet sources have the artwork, and encourage friends to submit favorable reviews. Also, provide an author's commentary or interview.
7. Sell the book on your website.
8. Offer the book for purchase whenever you acquire a speaking assignment.
9. Provide signed copies for local large booksellers, such as Barnes & Noble, and offer an author's signing at their convenience.
10. Send the book to local radio and television stations and affiliates.
11. Cite the book in your biographical information at the end of articles and in your introductions.
12. If you're teaching a course, assign the book as required reading if it is at all appropriate.

The only thing harder than commercially publishing a book is effectively marketing that book. You must accept that accountability yourself. The publisher will tell you one thing, but usually do another.

Some caveats:

- Don't rush to hire a public relations firm. Most of them charge a stiff retainer and don't perform all that well because they don't understand consulting or individual authors. I would not advise investing your budgeted money unless it's on a pay-for-performance basis.
- Lean heavily on the publisher's PR people. The squeaky wheel *does* get the attention from people whose limited resources can't possibly match the number of titles published over the course of the year. Make a pest out of yourself (you have absolutely nothing to lose).

## SOME OTHER VERY IMPORTANT ISSUES

It doesn't matter how many books you sell or how much you receive in royalties, and I know that sounds completely counterintuitive. However, the point in your publishing a book is establishing a brand and gaining clients. Naturally, the

## VIGNETTE

A mentoree of mine wrote a very nice book on customer service. The book went into the publisher's catalog, onto Amazon.com, and that was it, despite all the publisher questionnaires he completed and all the review copies he sent out.

Then we embarked on a more aggressive plan. He had friends and supporters write positive reviews on Amazon; he brought the book with him in bulk to all his public appearances; he placed the title in his email signature file and offered a discount; he gave a copy out for free when he spoke to whomever could first answer a trivia question; he secured reviews in local newspapers and trade association newsletters.

Gradually, word of mouth began to increase, and his book has become a modest success, remaining in print and generating consulting business as well as a second book contract.

Never rely on the publisher to promote. It's like a bank loan: When you really need it you can't get it, and when you don't need it, everyone is offering one.

wider spread the readership the better, but the key is to have the *right* readership. (Which is also why appearing on a mid-afternoon radio show for an hour is less attractive than a drive-time show for ten minutes, since your potential buyers are much more apt to be listening to the latter and working during the former.)

Get your book—and, therefore, your brand—in front of the right people, even for free. If you do make royalties, that's great. But a $350,000 consulting project resulting from a potential buyer receiving your book (and I've closed several of these from different books) is much more valuable than selling 10,000 books and making a few bucks on each. It doesn't even matter if the buyer has read the book; what matters is whether you're in front of the buyer as a result of the book and your brand recognition.

Eventually, your book will go out of print. There is a clause in virtually every publisher's contract calling for "reversion of rights," which means basically that if the publisher declares the book "out of print" you have the right to buy the film and printing resources at cost (a few hundred dollars) and print it yourself. That is a bargain, even if a print run of two thousand hard cover books costs you about $6,000 to $8,000. First, you'll now make about $15 or $18 per book if you sell them at $20 or $25; second, Amazon and other distributors will still sell them, with you as the publisher[4]; and third, you will have an inexpensive promotion tool for your brand, which you can continue to put in front of buyers, in the exact same format as the original (but without the publisher's name, although "originally published by . . ." nicely circumvents that restriction).

---

Once published, there's no reason to *ever* abandon a book, although you may want to update it from time to time. The only criterion is: Will the book continue to promote your brand or brands?

---

[4] I receive several hundred dollars every month just from Amazon.com, representing self-published books that they sell on my behalf.

## BRAND NEW LESSONS

You can't afford *not* to at least attempt to publish a book, and remember that, once published, ensuing works become easier and easier. (A female editor once told me at lunch that I had a "nice shelf," which almost caused my steak to make a return visit, until I realized that she was referring to my prior book output.) It's the first bold step that is the most difficult, but after that it is, indeed, downhill.

Organize your writing as you would any client project. Determine whether you will use an agent or try to directly influence an acquisitions editor. Use an orderly system to write over a finite period. Utilize daily reading and interactions to augment your work, using a manila folder system.

Most of all, promote your brand shamelessly throughout. In the worst case, an editor might request a bit less blatant promotion, but you never know until you try. In the meantime, say a few kind words about Guttenburg, who created a true miracle for us all.

# CHAPTER 5

# How to Conquer the Lecture Circuit

## *Using the Platform to Raise Your Brand*

With the exception of a commercially published book, professional speaking is the best mechanism to establish strong brands. I'm talking here of "professional" speaking and not merely "public" speaking. The latter is about civic events and Toastmasters clubs and volunteering; the former is about trade associations, management conferences, and significant fees.

Professional speaking has the following immediate advantages:

- Perception of quality—"you get what you pay for"
- Tacit third-party endorsement from the organizers, management, speakers bureau, etc.
- You've been hired to educate and develop the audience, not merely to hawk your services

- Peripheral coverage in other media of the event
- Audience acting as recommenders and word-of-mouth sources to others
- Significant income stream

Every consultant and entrepreneur today needs what are often called "platform skills," or presentation skills in any case, because we're often called on to make a marketing presentation, report our findings, apprise a management team, address the board or investors, conduct a workshop, and so forth.

## WHY PROFESSIONAL SPEAKING IS BRAND-EFFECTIVE (THE "REACH" OF THE SPEECH)

As you read this, whether on a weekend or weekday, there are probably close to 100,000 meetings requiring outside speakers being conducted in the United States alone.[1] The meetings are usually in one of these categories:

1. Corporate meetings of brief duration to education and develop management
2. Corporate training programs of longer duration to build specific skills among supervisors and managers
3. Small corporate retreats, offsite, for the purposes of establishing a marketing plan, strategy, growth policy, etc.
4. Public seminars run by independent training firms
5. Trade association meetings and conventions attended by representatives of members or member firms
6. Government-sponsored meetings to educate business people, apprise the public of regulations, etc.

---

[1]This is an unscientific estimate, but if you're in doubt visit or call any major hotel of conference center and ask about an average month's bookings. There are easily 1,000 meetings a day in New York City, Chicago, and Los Angeles alone, even if North Dakota might pull down the average a bit.

7. Third-party meetings, in which a firm—say, Coldwell Banker Relocation Services—is running educational meetings for its own customers and vendors to forge better alliances[2]

---

> In the face of every high-tech advance and concern about travel expenses, meetings—and the speakers who are an ineluctable part of them—have proliferated.

If 1 percent of those 100,000 meetings are relevant to your brand, it means that there are 1,000 meetings a day, 7,000 a week, 30,000 a month, over a third of a million a year that are of branding potential for you.

If you were to speak just twice a month—at only one of the 30,000 meetings that might be appropriate for your brand—and there were an average audience of one hundred people at each meeting, you would be reaching 2,400 people per year, who in turn might tell another three people each about your message, and so on and so forth. After speaking for several years, and/or speaking more often, your word-of-mouth brand effectiveness has reached hundreds of thousands of people who have some affinity for the services and benefits you provide. It's small wonder that, after a couple of successful years on the lecture circuit, speakers find themselves pursued based on their word of mouth. The "gravity" has taken hold.

## PREPARING YOUR MESSAGE: INSIDER TIPS ON OUTSTANDING SPEAKING

The secret to preparing any speech is to organize it *from the audience's perspective and interests.* Don't attempt to tell people everything you know, or even what you think they should know. Instead, determine what your audience needs to immediately improve their personal and/or professional lives *using your brand.*

---

[2]I'm strictly dealing with interactive, "live" meetings, and not the extensive network of video-conferences, teleconferences, and Internet conferences.

If you are professional and have any kind of brand, you will be a well-received speaker because people believe that you should be good, want you to be good and, if you're not good, they fear it may be their own fault for "not getting it."

I once strode into the back of a hall deliberately having missed 99 percent of a nationally known but simply dreadful speaker. As I waited in the shadows during his closing, I noticed two women who were sound asleep, heads on the table, arms sprawled at their sides.

When the speaker concluded and received the stereotypical, albeit undeserved, standing ovation, the women were awakened, jumped to their feet, and began to applaud.

As the room began to empty, I approached them and asked how they liked the speaker.

"He was fabulous," they gushed.

"Which part did you like best?" I innocently inquired.

"Oh, it was all great," they assured me as they gathered their belongings and hurried off.

Sometimes you just have to be present; you don't have to be good, but it sure helps.

Here's an example: If your brand is "Sales Acceleration," don't overly emphasize how you formulated your approach or the beauty of the sixth step in the process. Focus on the individual person in the audience who will be able to make more money through higher commissions based on larger, more frequent sales. If your brand is "Capturing Opportunity," don't stress the need to "raise the bar" (which is a platitude at this point), but stress the chance to reinvent oneself and to try new endeavors without excessive risk.

So, here are Alan's quick methods to establish a speech even if you've never professionally spoken before:

1. Choose a theme tied to your brand
2. Orient the entire speech around benefits to the listener
3. Create a powerful two-minute opening
4. Organize your content around a forty-five-minute main segment
5. Create a powerful five-minute closing
6. Create visual aids and handouts to support point 4

That's it. You can lengthen or shorten as needed, but those are the ingredients for a solid one-hour talk.[3]

## 1. Choose a Theme Tied to Your Brand

The speech is pointless for you if it doesn't promote your brand(s). If your brand is "The Team Builder," then title the speech "The Team Builder Approach to Higher Performance." If your brand is your own name, then "Alan Weiss on Team Building" might be the right slant.

## 2. Orient the Entire Speech Around Benefits to the Listener

Write some initial thoughts down about benefits to the audience. These must be outputs, not inputs—in other words, "a more productive workforce" is an output, but "creating a team environment" is an input (the latter is of no worth unless it produces the former). Try to create a list of a dozen or more specific benefits to the audience. This will be useful in marketing your speech as well as in formulating the content.

> Effective speeches have a sturdy, simple architecture, which creates an attractive structure as well as one that can withstand the stress of the elements.

[3]And those of you already speaking professionally could do worse than to review your presentations in light of this template.

## 3. Create a Powerful Two-Minute Opening

People generally decide how much of their attention to grant you within the first two minutes of your talk. Psychologically speaking, they will begin to make notes, or to tune you out and browse through their conference literature, in a very brief time. The good news is that, once you've "hooked" them, it's tough to lose them again. The bad news is that, once you've lost them, it's impossible to "rehook" them.

The answer to this is in a powerful opening. Your powerful opening should use one of the following:

- Personal story or anecdote
- Statistics
- Demonstration
- Example
- History or historical facts
- Projections about the future

I heard a speaker whose topic was health start by stating that the total smoking-related deaths in the United States alone equaled three fully loaded 747 jets crashing with no survivors *every day of the year.* "What do you think the public reaction to that would be?" he asked. Every person in the house was riveted on his next words.

I usually begin with a personal story or anecdote, always self-effacing, because the audience can relate to them, the laugh is on me, and I can then segue into my main points. For example, I often begin with a story that has me treading water next to an overturned sailboat where the water was only five feet deep, and I continued to tread until someone walked over to me. My point: "Perception is reality, and if we think the water is deep, we keep treading until we're exhausted, when we could have simply walked away. How deep is the water you're in right now?" I then go on to talk about empowerment.

Develop an opener that gains attention quickly and permits you to smoothly transfer to your main points. Do not open with a "joke," and do not open with a story that you've heard somewhere, because a great many people in the audience have probably heard it as well. Your speech must be personally yours.

# 4. Organize Your Content Around a Forty-Five-Minute Main Segment

Choose five or ten main points you want to convey. Use the initial list of audience benefits you generated above. Select the most potent, and make them your key points. Simply divide to determine how much time to spend on each. If you have nine, you have about five minutes per point; if you have five, then you have about nine minutes per point.

Make your points clear to the audience: "I've found that in 'capturing opportunity' there are five keys to empowerment. Here is number one. . . ." Audiences love numbered lists and sequential steps. They also serve to keep you focused and in proper sequence.

Support each of your points with examples, statistics, and/or anecdotes. The fewer points (for example, five in forty-five minutes) the more support you'll need for each.[4] If one point is "Decisions must be forced to the lowest supervisory levels," then your supporting points (in terms of audience benefit) might include:

- Costs are lowered when successive levels aren't involved
- Customers are satisfied the first time at the point of contact (insert here a story about frustrated customers)
- Decisions passed upward are seldom different from what would have been decided at the front line (cite statistics here)
- Delays in response result in lost repeat business (cite your own research)

Keep your talk conversational. Use self-effacing humor. The audience *wants the speech to be a success.* No one wants to be a part of a poor presentation.

[4]I know that this method seems heavily oriented to time, and that's because the speech must fit into a given context. Hence, your job is to take excellent points and tailor them to time demands, not to throw everything you know into the mix and allow the entire meeting schedule to suffer from your prolixity.

This "main body" of the speech can be continually edited and improved as time goes by and you learn more, or as you want to keep it more contemporary. This is where "tinkering" can take place. You might reduce or increase your main points. But at least the car is built, and you're merely adding some fuel or polishing the chassis.

## 5. Create a Powerful Five-Minute Closing

Too many speeches sort of evaporate away at the end. A good closing will provide a memorable impression of your brand, as well as create a "call to action" so that your speech has pragmatic utility and isn't just a theoretical construct that no one can use the next day.

There's nothing wrong with beginning the ending with "in summary" or "let's summarize," which alerts the audience to the fact that they'd better pay close attention *and* that you intend to hit your ending time. (It's always better to finish a few minutes early rather than a few minutes late. Once your ending time has come and gone, listening drops off by more than 50 percent in my estimation, and sometimes attendance will, also.)

You can summarize your key points ("We've discussed five methods of empowerment, which are . . ."), end with a call to action ("Tomorrow, demand that your employees make three decisions that they would normally send to your desk . . ."), and/or with a story *that reinforces your points* and is not just thrown in because you like it. Here's the test: Just like a tune that people hum, what words, phrases, or ideas do you want them to be mulling over and discussing as they walk out of your presentation? They should be highlighted in your closing, whatever they are.

## 6. Create Visual Aids and Handouts to Support Point 4

There are no rules about handouts and visual aids other than rule 1: If handouts and/or visual aids enhance the learning and reinforce your brand, then use them. If they don't, then don't. One of the most overdone speaking aids these days is PowerPoint®, and it has become technology for technology's sake.

In the course of an hour's speech, you seldom need visual aids (as opposed to a longer session in which they are needed for diversity and variety). However, they can be quite effective when underscoring a point. And in light of the fact that many people learn better visually, the more complicated your topic, the more visual aids are useful—*so long as the visual aids simplify and don't add to the complication.*

For small groups, overhead slides, easels, white boards, and similar aids are fine. For larger groups, 35mm slides or computer projection are required. For huge groups, computer projection is a must, sometimes with screens around the hall. Keep in mind that projection devices require dimmed lighting, which can be a problem.

Handouts were once de rigueur, but today you can refer people to your website if you have articles, copies of your presentation, and so forth available. However, handouts are very useful in any case for reinforcing your brand, so they are generally advisable. *Hint:* Aside from text and copies of your presentation, you might want to create and distribute small plastic or laminated cards that contain your key points *and* your branding. These tend to remain on people's desktops or in their planners, a constant reminder of you and your brand. A copy of both sides of mine appears on the next page.

> Like articles or books, speeches don't have to be perfect, but merely successful. Don't spend days trying to create the Gettysburg Address. In fact, it only took Lincoln a few minutes and the back of an envelope to create that, so how much time can you need?

In summary, creating a speech around each of your brands from the viewpoint of "what's in it for the listener" is a key ingredient in brand publicity and perpetuation. No one else can sell your brand like you can, so you might as well learn to get good at it.

## THE ELEMENTS OF A POWERFUL DELIVERY

You're probably good enough to deliver your message right now. Think of all those horrible executive presentations you've had to sit through as a consultant, where you debate giving all your fees back if they'll just let you out of that boring talk by the CEO. Just a modicum of platform skills are needed to set you

"Empowerment means being able to make decisions which influence the outcome of your work."

—Alan Weiss, Ph.D.

### Focus on Five Factors

1. **Keep raising the bar**
   *Innovation* over problem solving

2. **Achieve results and outcomes**
   Means are less important than *ends*

3. **Empower: power doesn't corrupt**
   *Powerlessness* creates bureaucracy

4. **People only believe what they see**
   *Examplars,* not banners in the hall

5. **Perception is reality**
   Wear the *other person's* shoes

*Thanks for attending!*
Alan Weiss, Ph.D.
Summit Consulting Group, Inc.
Box 1009
East Greenwich, RI 02818
800/766-7935
Fax: 401/884-5068
e-mail: info@summitconsulting.com
home page: http://www.summitconsulting.com

apart from the crowd. (And, incidentally, Toastmasters is a good, safe training ground, although their types of speeches are more for contests and high school rallies than they are for businesses. But they will help with any initial stage fright and in working out the mechanics.)

First, no speech should be memorized, and notes are perfectly fine. The only things that should be memorized are the two-minute opening, so that you can confidently begin and capture attention, and the five-minute closing, which is simply a summary and call to action that should be dynamic.

Use notes that are large and in bullet form—never write out or script a speech. If you use visual aids, they can serve as your outline. I've often simply spoken about the slides without a note at all. Bullet points allow you to follow a sequence *but also to talk conversationally, the key to professional speaking, since you won't be reading text.* It's better to struggle for a word and make an error in conversation with the audience than it is to bore them to tears with a prerecorded message.

Write out your introduction and demand that the introducer read it verbatim, which will give you a strong "entrance" and a familiar one every time. (Most introducers are plain awful.) Take a moment after the applause to gather yourself and wait for silence, then begin calmly on your set two-minute opening. After that you can refer to your bullet point notes as needed. (Remember, large type: There are often lighting problems.)

Use a wireless lavaliere mike, which frees up your hands and allows you to move around without tripping over wires. Use your hands for expression. Don't be cemented behind the podium. And here's the greatest delivery hint of all: Smile. Smiling sends a friendly tone to the audience, says that you're not nervous, actually relaxes facial muscles and tension, and psychologically will boost your spirits. (Don't smile at bad news, but I think you get the idea.)

Ask someone to be your timer if you're not comfortable timing yourself or you're uneasy with the speech length in your rehearsals, and adjust your pace accordingly. If you take questions, which is always a good idea, do so near the end but not at the very end. Save your closing for after the questions, so that you end powerfully. When you take questions, remember this "3R" formula:

- Restate the question so that everyone can hear it and you have time to consider an answer (and to make sure you got it right).

- Respond to the question as concisely and directly as you can. ("I don't know and I'll have to get back to you on that one," is a perfectly fine answer, and superior to tap dancing any day.)
- Review with the inquirer to ensure that you responded to the question. ("Did I answer your question?" "Was that response satisfactory?")

With any hostile questions, use only the first two and do not apply the third, instead looking to another questioner or going to your summary to avoid any one-on-one debate.

Remember to periodically include your brand in a "soft" manner, for example, "When I was doing my initial research into 'The Power of Empowerment,' I learned that in organizations such as yours. . . ."

Audiences want to participate in a successful speech. They are overwhelmingly in your corner. That being the case, here's a piece of advice: Don't lose them.

Practice your delivery with a cassette recorder, and try to have your early talks taped live so that you can critique how you've done. You'll be able to rearrange, insert, and delete and, in short order, you'll have a speech and a delivery which will stand you proud.

# TURBO-MARKETING YOUR SPEAKING EFFORTS

Use the synergy of the "gravity" effect to market your speaking efforts. The most important aspects are to provide marketing materials directly oriented toward professional speaking and to be recognized as a speaker.

## Checklist: Speaker Marketing Support "Musts"

Here are the speaker-specific marketing materials you'll need:

### A Sample Audio and/or Video of at Least Thirty Minutes
You can arrange this in one of three ways:

1. When a group does hire you to speak, arrange (with the group's permission) for a taping team to be present. Some groups have their own facility and staff and may agree to do this for you.
2. Offer your services to a group for free, in exchange for the right to tape the proceedings.
3. Hire a private room in a club or restaurant, invite thirty of your friends to a free lunch or dinner, with the understanding that first they are to be a great audience for you. Don't laugh. This method has been used by many speakers who are currently earning five figures a speech. I still use the approach for some product videos I create.

You can usually obtain a good audio track from a digital video recording, killing two birds with one stone. Make sure your practice has created a powerful speech, that the mikes pick up audience reaction, and that you don't date the taping by mentioning current events or specific dates. Also, have a professional prepare the room—I watched one videotape that had the speaker in front of a large mirror, which, of course, reflected the camera, the staff, the audience, and every other distraction imaginable.

This is the tape you'll send to prospects and bureaus, so have it carefully edited, place a voice-over at the beginning and end, and place your contact information at the conclusion. Create a nice label and box.

*Warning: Try not to use professional video services that specialize in speaker videos, since every product looks exactly alike and undifferentiated. You're better off with a few flaws and honest mistakes than you are with vanilla perfection.*

## Testimonials About Your Speaking Effectiveness

The best way to obtain these early is to speak at Rotary, Kiwanis, Lions, Elks, parent-teacher associations, chambers of commerce, and similar service and community groups. When an audience member tells you afterward how enjoyable your speech was, ask frankly and conversationally for a testimonial: "You know, testimonials are my stock in trade in this profession, and if you'd be kind enough to put that on your letterhead, I'd greatly appreciate it. Here's my card." That person is often a vice president at a bank, general manager at a retailer, or editor at a newspaper. You're not claiming them as clients, but you will gain a testimonial from a bank officer quite legitimately.

> The best way to start speaking is to start speaking. Don't wait for the "perfect" opportunity. Exploit the very next opportunity.

## Adapt Your Press Kit and Other Publicity Accordingly

You don't need a separate press kit for your speaking activities, but you do need to make them apparent in your present press kit. Include the testimonials. Include the results generated by your speaking. Enclose the audiotape for prospects when appropriate. Organize your press kit so that even consulting prospects can see that you're an accomplished speaker and, therefore, even more of an authority in your field.

Create a separate area on your website that addresses your speaking activities and experience.[5] If you send out newsletters, include your availability and your upcoming speaking appearances. This is what I mean by using the synergy of the rest of your gravitational field.

## Speakers Bureaus

In addition to the standard marketing techniques, there is an additional avenue available in speaking, which doesn't really have an equivalent in consulting, and that is the speakers bureau. A bureau essentially represents scores (or even hundreds) of speakers and takes a commission of about 25 percent of the speaker's fee for placing the speaker at clients. There are pros and cons to this approach.

*The Pros of Speakers Bureaus.* Speakers bureaus are advantageous for the following reasons:

---

[5]*Note:* NEVER place a fee schedule of your speaking in any publicity or promotional materials. Fees can and should vary based on your value to the client, no different from consulting assignments. Most people who are solely professional speakers don't understand this concept at all.

- They can place you in markets and with clients you would not normally be able to reach
- The good ones can negotiate good deals, and will position you, alone, as the best speaker for that assignment
- They tend to keep placing good speakers and can form a residual body of business for you
- They can keep you apprised of what marketing elements you need to improve or create

*The Cons of Speakers Bureaus.*   The disadvantages include:

- Some bureaus simply offer a half-dozen or more speakers to a client with no positioning, since they get a commission no matter who is chosen. In fact, some use lower-fee, newer speakers as "fodder," which enables them to place their higher-fee (higher commission) veterans.
- Bureaus take 25 percent of your fee, and some take 30 percent. Some of them will actually hold your money, despite being paid themselves, until well after the speech.
- Many bureaus are paranoid about not trusting speakers and demand that the speaker not talk independently to the client (which prevents a relationship from forming) and require that speakers "sterilize" materials and even websites, so that the speaker contact data does not appear anywhere at all! This does not a healthy partnership make.
- Many bureaus, on top of their 25 percent share, want the speaker to invest in marketing activities (such as mailings and websites), despite that fact that the commission should be covering that marketing.[6]
- Finally, many bureaus are nothing more than dating services trying to get lucky, simply asking the speaker to send materials to someone they heard is searching for a speaker and then wanting their cut if they get lucky. Many "bureaus" are actually that: a bureau with a Rolodex in someone's bedroom.

There are some excellent bureaus and some truly dreadful ones and, like bank loans, they're easier to get when you don't really need them. The best way

---

[6]Here's the latest: Many bureaus now charge speakers just to review their materials to assess whether or not they will deign to represent them. Will chutzpah never end?

to secure the representation of a first-rate speakers bureau is by networking in through a colleague already represented by them.

---

> The relationship with a bureau must be one of partners helping each other. No true partner makes demands of the other and expects none to be made in return.

## THE MAGIC OF SETTING HIGH FEES (THE GOOD STUFF)

Set your speaking fees the way you would your consulting fees—base them on the value derived by the client and your contribution to that value. You must understand the following dynamic.

No one is worth what he or she receives for a brief keynote or even a lengthier workshop. Whether a celebrity speaker at $75,000, a well-known business speaker at $10,000, or a lesser known but effective speaker at $5,000, none is worth that amount based on the time in front of the audience. *However,* a speaker's ability to take his or her past (experiences, education, travels, learning, values, socialization, work, hobbies, observations, successes, failures, and so forth) and use a current intervention (keynote, workshop, facilitation, seminar, etc.) to create long-lived client results (improved morale, increased sales, better customer service, reduced attrition, etc.) is worth a huge amount.

*The above dynamic is not appreciated by most speakers nor most bureaus, which are wrapped up in fee schedules and charge by time unit.* Your ability, with a consultant's background, to understand this relationship is key to charging correctly based on the assignment and attendant value.

Enter into speech negotiations the same way you would consulting negotiations: Establish objectives, measures of success, and value to the client, then provide options across a fee range that represents your contribution to that value. Even in a keynote, you can offer options:

- The keynote delivered for forty-five minutes
- Interview customers first and include their comments

I was asked to speak for a day on value-based fees to a high-tech firm in San Diego, which was mired in low fee hourly billing schedules. There were thirty people in the room and when I said, "Good morning," the CEO immediately interrupted.

"Before Alan goes any further," he said to his team, "he's agreed to spend a day with us, 8:30 to 5:00, to interact with us about value-based fees. If this were you, what would you charge me for the day as a new customer?"

"I think a thousand," said one sales person, and another said, "I'd go fifteen hundred." (They were all multiplying hourly rates times the hours I'd be with them.) "Fifteen hundred sounds kind of high," said a third, "so maybe somewhere in between."

"Well," replied the CEO as he sat down again, "he's charging us *eighteen thousand dollars,* so I want you all to listen up!!"

- Interview employees and include their comments
- Conduct a breakout session after the keynote for more intimate questions and answers among a select part of the audience
- Conduct a benchmarking study to use in the keynote
- Provide special access to your website for the audience

I could go on and on. You can provide options for any kind of speaking engagement if you understand what your client may need. The mistake most speakers make is that they "bundle" rather than "unbundle," throwing in everything but the kitchen sink to justify what they want to charge for that hour, *since they feel guilty about the fee they are charging for that hour,* not understanding the dynamic I've explained above. The last several paragraphs are the key to high-fee speaking, period. It doesn't matter how long you've been speaking or how often.

People believe they get what they pay for, which is what I call "the Mercedes-Benz syndrome." No one expects much from a $1,000 speaker, but people will fill the hall to hear a $10,000 speaker. What's the difference? Nine thousand dollars.

I happened to meet a full-time professional speaker at a hotel pool who didn't know who I was. He bragged to me that he was speaking at 150 dates a year for a fee of $2,000 each. That means that he's almost constantly on the road to earn a gross of $300,000. I told him he could double his fees and cut his travel in half, or raise his fees to a very modest $3,500 and create an additional quarter of a million dollars *in profit*. He looked at me like I was crazy. He was 58 years old. He didn't get it, and he never would.

Bureaus will demand fee schedules. I suggest that you create a fee for a keynote (up to ninety minutes), a workshop (up to three hours), and a seminar (a full day). That immediately provides some options. However, I strongly recommend that your policy be that you negotiate the fee with the buyer, so that you can offer options such as those listed earlier; the bureau will only benefit from your ability to raise fees.

> I've often been paid five figures for a brief speech with the client incredibly grateful, because the client and I were both focused on the results generated in the audience, not on the amount of time I was physically present. This is of tremendous help when consulting projects ensue which are also value-based.

## EXPLOITING SUCCESS

My consulting, speaking, and publishing careers have blended together, and there's no reason why yours shouldn't go in the same direction. I've often been asked to address a company's management team after conducting a consulting project, or been asked to begin consulting after people have heard me speak, or been invited in to do both after someone has read my books. (And, of course, after appearing as a speaker or consulting on a project, there are many requests for my books and tapes.)

The commonality across the products and services is your brand. The easiest way for people to gracefully and intuitively accept a consultant as a speak-

At a medical conference hosted in New England (and as reported in the *New England Journal of Medicine* several years ago), one of the presenters who was well-advertised failed to show up. His session was, therefore, cancelled.

Conference organizers were both bemused and shocked to find that, in the overall conference feedback, participants gave the no-show one of the highest evaluations of any speaker at the entire conference.

In an earlier vignette we pointed out that sometimes you just have to show up. Apparently, even that isn't always necessary.

er, an author as a consultant, a speaker as an author, and so on, is a transcending brand identity. I'm happy to take Tylenol, a brand I trust, in pill, caplets, gel caps, or other configurations. The name Gillette represents quality in a great variety of men's toiletry products. Ferrari licenses its logo to a range of clothing.

Make sure that your brand (or brands) is constant and prominent. Catchphrases, key findings, logos, powerful imagery, and other brand identifiers should be applied across media and across your services. If your brand is your name, then that, too, should be prominent, which is why you find configurations such as "Paul Newman's . . ." or "Andrew Lloyd Weber's. . . ." Personal name brands become so powerful that Tom Clancy has lent his name to books he didn't even write, which is a rather extreme (and precarious and ethically questionable) use of personal name branding.

I've found that professional speaking is a lucrative part of my practice, but it's not a sideline. It is an intrinsic part, which can generate revenue on its own, but even more importantly creates a platform for my brand to be exposed to tens of thousands of buyers of potential, six-figure consulting projects. I've sold major projects to people who called me after having heard me speak for free at an industry event or public forum.

One key trick of the trade, combining your consulting and speaking efforts: Casually ask your consulting clients what trade associations they belong to, and what their role is in them. Many of them, finding out that I was also a professional speaker, introduced me to the program chairs of their trade association conferences. Some, like Merck, have even sponsored me (paid the speaking fee) so that I could appear at a trade association that couldn't otherwise afford me, gaining them some nice publicity as well.

(I remember asking the CEO of an insurance company I had worked with for several years if his company belonged to any major trade associations. He said, "Of course. In fact, I'm the program chair for next year's meeting of the American Council of Life Insurance." Next thing I knew, I was the keynote speaker. I simply had never asked, and he had never known.)

---

View your brand as an umbrella, within which you provide consulting services, a range of products, speaking services, newsletters and print materials, etc. You don't sell your brand. Your brand enables you to sell a variety of synergistic products and services.

## BRAND NEW LESSONS

Next to a major book, the speaking circuit is the most effective method to broaden the reach of your brand. If you're already doing some speaking, develop it into a major aspect of your business and your branding. If you've never done it, you can hit the ground running simply by preparing a strong message, delivering it well, marketing aggressively, and exploiting your successes.

Provide options and be flexible on your fees, basing them on value and not on time. Use only those bureaus with which you feel a strong partnering attitude. Adjust your publicity and materials to highlight your speaking as well as your consulting and other activities.

It isn't my intent to make every reader into an expert professional speaker, but it is my intent to insist that you at least examine this alternative as a sound and pragmatic branding strategy. You may be uncomfortable speaking, but it's important for all of us to step outside of our comfort zones.

Speaking is a key to brand awareness. If we don't toot our own horns, there isn't any music.

# CHAPTER 6

# The Twelve Myths of 21st Century Branding

## I Didn't Walk in Here and I'm Not Leaving

I once worked with a manager who consistently got drunk at parties and, when asked to leave, would state boldly: "I didn't walk in here, and I'm not leaving." What do you do with that kind of mysterious logic? It usually bought him a few more minutes of drinking.

Similarly, what do we do with the strange and bizarre advice that surrounds branding, especially branding for the consulting profession? Unfortunately, when an idea takes hold a plethora of advice soon follows, most of it questionable. After all, if every "Get Rich Tomorrow" book actually was valid, there would be no need for any future books on the subject because everyone would, in fact, already be rich. Similarly, how adept can those stockbrokers be who call you at home at the worst possible time in the evening? If they really knew what they were talking about, wouldn't they be wealthy from their own investments and so sought out by important investors that they wouldn't need to solicit business by begging people on the phone?

Consequently, it's as important to decide who and what *not* to listen to as it is to determine what makes sense for you in terms of your brands. While some sources carp on a single alternative which favors their expertise ("the Internet is the sole mechanism for global branding"), others simply use their standard approach and "convert" it to the latest fad ("how to use personality profiling in branding"). In fact, branding is not a fad, since it's been used in one form or another for millennia (and most traditional product marketing accelerated with the advent of television a half century ago), nor is its effectiveness confined to a single medium, since branding reflects your competencies and authority, not the distribution channel.

I've organized the mythology into twelve categories, which follow. You might already know of others or be able to permutate these into another dozen. Here's the acid test: If a source claims a magic route or royal route to branding, ask yourself whether you know of an exception, whether you can undermine the logic, and/or whether you can detect unsubstantiated bias. If the answer is "yes" to any of those tests, ignore the advice. Here are a dozen types of advice you can ignore immediately.

> Branding is a conceptual marketing strategy. Therefore, the options to utilize the approach are usually circumscribed only by your own competence and innovation.

## THE MYTHS

### Myth #1: A Tight Intellectual Argument Is Sufficient

Logic makes people think and emotion makes them act. I'm tempted to move to Myth #2, but I'll provide some additional support for my case.

Ask any insurance salesperson and he or she will tell you how valid this phenomenon is. When you make a pitch about the horror of estate taxes, for example, and the fact that they can be significantly reduced if one buys a large insurance policy today and utilizes it as a complex trust instrument, most people's eyes glaze over. (In fact, those premiums for individuals leaving large estates can be upwards of $50,000 a year for twenty years in some of these estate plans.)

However, once the agent introduces the fact that the potential insured's children are the ones being protected, and that the wicked government will take over half of the carefully and hard-won estate now being created by someone who, him- or herself, never had such a legacy, the tone of the conversation changes. Protecting two children from the government's future action is a much more significant emotional impetus than is the logic of cold numbers appearing on a computer spread sheet.

And this despite the fact that the children will be over fifty years old themselves and, presumably, earning their own decent livings, by the time the estate threat and insurance protection are triggered by the insured's and spouse's deaths!

Don't peg your brand to purely cerebral justification or appeal. The phrase "because it's right for your organization" will always be less effective than one that says "because you'll sleep more confidently when you're not at the office." Many years ago, when Kodak finally discovered it had serious competition in an industry it thought it had a divine right to exclusively control, it responded with the fascinating breakthrough that it wasn't in the film business any more, but rather in the business of preserving memories. After all, do you really want to trust those once-in-a-lifetime photos of your daughter's wedding to any other film? This was brilliant stuff.

When you create brochure, print, electronic, or other materials, ensure that your appeal is at least partially directed at the visceral level. Complex sales models are nice (and always intrigue the creators), but some assurance about finally not worrying about meeting your sales quota at 11:30 p.m. on December 31 will generally attract people's attention with more vigor.

*Key: Listen to the customer's heart.*

---

Take a moment to consider what appeals reach you the most rapidly and effectively. After all, you're "the buyer" for many other firms. If you're honest, you'll find that the great majority of unplanned purchases you make are impulse buys or "pitches" that appeal to your gut. Your own buyers are no different.

## Myth #2: You Must Analyze the Environment for Need

If branding were simply a matter of scanning—or even meticulously parsing—the environment, most people would be able to do it superbly well with the aid of templates and specialized consultants. But since most people can't do it well and those templates don't really exist, there must be some other factors at work.

In fact, the best way to brand is by asking "What if?" and not "What is?" The act of creating brands must be future-oriented. Many people emphasize taking advantage of current fads and movements, and that advice is excellent—if you're still living in the 1960s. Once upon a time, fads lasted long enough to be publicized, studied, and exploited within the next year or so. Today, fads are ephemeral, with the half-life of one of those non-natural elements that scientists create in cyclotrons. Nanoseconds are suddenly useful measuring devices. In "the old days," even Nehru jackets and midi-skirts lasted long enough for everyone to poke fun at them and brag how they didn't purchase them (in the same manner that there is apparently no one in the country who voted for Nixon). Today, a poorly received style doesn't make it to the retail stores and movies that don't receive decent previews go directly to videotape.

Today, in the electronic age, fads and movements come and go with tremendous velocity and acceleration. By the time a book is conventionally written and published—often a time period of nine months or more—its subject may well have disappeared into history's upstairs closet.

Brands must anticipate the future. Akio Morita at Sony created not only the Walkman, but the entire "industry" of mobile music devices, by considering what future need he could create, and not what current "want" he should cater to (and against the best advice of his designers and engineers). Many early, successful product brands associated themselves, often with a breathtaking leap of faith, with the space age and scientific breakthrough. (Hence, "new" is one of the most common adjectives in many product brands.)

Create your brands with future need in mind. Consider how they'll appear in a year's time and how flexible they are to changing times. A team-building approach that accents diversity and emphasizes front-line decision making isn't likely to go out of style any time soon. But a team-building approach that stresses personality profiling and outdoor games might be laughable next week.

*Key: Don't look around in awareness, but rather ahead in anticipation.*

Noted writer and management thinker Russ Ackoff related once that a famous dog food company had invested tens of millions in a new, nutritious, highly promoted canned food. Unfortunately, it was a tremendous bomb, an unmitigated disaster, and heads were going to roll.

At the "accountability" meeting called by the CEO to determine how the brand failed and who was at fault, the two dozen top executives sat glumly while the CEO lambasted the lot. Then he shouted, "WHO IS RESPONSIBLE?!!"

"Well, it wasn't us," said the vice president of R&D. "We performed exhaustive tests and the nutrients can't be found in any other product at twice the price. The American Veterinary Association endorsed the brand for the first time in its history."

"Don't look at us," stammered the vice president of marketing. "We created print and broadcast ads that won awards. Our testing with the public in focus groups was the most comprehensive we've ever done."

"We worked ourselves out," said the vice president of sales. "Our field force was trained for a week on this single brand, we raised compensation rates, and we provided every sales aid imaginable."

"Well," said the CEO, "are we saying that no one was at fault? No one wants to take accountability?"

A lone hand went up in the rear of the room, and the CEO recognized a management intern whose name he couldn't remember. "Yes, son, what is it?"

"I think I know the reason for the failure, sir," mumbled the intern.

"Yes, yes, okay, speak up, what do you think it was?"

"The dogs just didn't like the stuff."

Trends and movements have a bell-curve configuration. Most people create a brand at what is really the beginning of the down slope. But don't congratulate yourself by creating one at the peak. The best branding occurs about two-thirds of the way up the up slope.

## Myth #3: Clever Catch Phrases and Adages Are Sufficient

This myth might be the converse of the first one. Emotion does make people act, but the emotion has to be connected with a real, perceived need (either already in existence or created, as with the example of Akio Morita), and not some abstract, unrelated concept.

When the Infiniti automobile was introduced years ago, following the already successful Lexus to market in an age infatuated with presumed Japanese quality, it embarked on a novel brand approach. Infiniti advertising did not mention or depict the automobile at all. Instead, the ads in both print and broadcast media showed Zen-like settings or rocks and waterfalls, highly aesthetic, and merely included the name "Infiniti."

Well, consumers didn't know what on earth was being pitched and actually became suspicious of a car that its manufacturer wouldn't show. Infiniti began in a deep hole, which it still hasn't climbed out of. (Infiniti is not profitable today, and every year there are rumors of its impending doom.)

There has to be a "connection" for brand appeals to work, even on the emotional level. FedEx and its original brand of "absolutely, positively has to get there the next day" appealed to every business person with urgent needs to please the customer or the boss, every one of whom had been undone at one time or another by the U.S. Postal Service.[1]

Your brand can be bolstered by cute phrases and witty sayings, but it

---

[1]Not long ago, a postal clerk told me "the guys in the back" had one of my books and were enjoying it. "How did they get it?" I asked. "Oh, it just showed up one day," said the clerk, never even thinking that it no doubt fell out of one of my mailings that they had flung around the sorting area!

nonetheless has to be relevant for your presumed buyer. Therefore, think carefully about who that *future* buyer is, what the buyer's concerns will be, and what the buyer's improved condition would look like. *Then* you can create the connection to the buyer's world.

And don't forget that clever phrases and funny situations are only alternatives, not mandatory aspects of branding. If you're an expert witness, or you provide consulting in the area of plant safety, you might want to tread lightly in the humor area.

---

We do remember clever phrases. But when consumers actually repeated the stock phrase, "It's Miller time," they proceeded to order Budweiser. It's more important to have a visceral connection with your brand than an intellectual one.

---

*Key: Don't worry about being funny. Worry about being useful.*

## Myth #4: Brands Are Developed over a Long Period of Time

Product brands such as Ivory Soap or Tide detergent are decades old. But Amazon.com, Yahoo, and even Apple are certainly not. The Palm Pilot occurred overnight. Even in the non-technical arena, Virgin Airlines developed a brand (as did Southwest) very quickly and in the face of huge, long-established competition.

We've all been subject to those ubiquitous CD ROMs provided for free by AOL, which have been instrumental in brand awareness and growth. Because of today's electronic age, and because traditional "word of mouth" is, in many cases, "speed of electronics," brand identities can be created and spread in a matter of days.

When I created a new newsletter and workshop series called "Balancing Act: Blending Life, Work, and Relationships," I had entered a field I wasn't known in and had no prior history in. However, I launched the newsletter using fewer than one hundred email addresses in my files, and grew to over two thousand subscribers in under twelve months. My first workshop drew a capacity crowd within ninety days, advertised strictly in my new and traditional newsletters and by word of mouth.

Today's extrapolation of news and new events can, literally, create a worldwide following within a week. The landmark Apple 1984 commercial aired during the Super Bowl launched the company into the big time, just as CNN's immediate and onsite coverage of the Gulf War metamorphosed it into a major television news competitor.

You have the capacity and resources to brand in "real time." The trick is to utilize the "gravitational field" as it relates to speed and your brand's features. As a rule, speaking, publishing, Internet sites, newsletters, ads and listings, and word-of-mouth networking are the best alternatives (and are mutually reinforcing) to launch a brand quickly and efficiently.

Consequently, make sure your brand is exactly right and tested before you launch it, because it's hard to retrieve! The most time should be invested in the preparation and creation, because the dissemination will take the least time of all. The speed of today's communication will spread an ineffective branding attempt just as rapidly as an effective one.

*Key: Plan for effectiveness and impact, because the speed will take care of itself.*

---

Many consultants have gained "negative brands" because communications and word of mouth aren't restricted to only positive messages we control. Your public image will be disseminated, like it or not, so your ongoing actions and results are constantly contributing to, or detracting from, your image.

## Myth #5: Brands Must Be Honed for Specific, Defined Targets

Consider concepts such as life-long learning, two-income families, retirement leading to second careers, mobile life styles, quality of life, zero inflation, zero unemployment, downsizing, reengineering, and healthy life styles. These are not traditional demographic categories, not easily identifiable social slices. Our buyers are not what they used to be and we might as well get used to it.

Do you really care whether your phone carrier is MCI, AT&T, Sprint, or Old Mother Hubbard Wireless? Probably not. Those brands are less important than cost, convenience, accessibility, and peripheral features such as call waiting or caller ID. Are you really buying a computer brand, or an Intel chip, or a processing speed? Do you choose an airline by name, or by flight schedule or frequent flyer program? (Most studies currently show that the determinant is the appeal of the frequent flyer program if routes are similar.) For that matter, look at who's flying today versus twenty-five years ago: Then it was business people, well attired and mostly male; today, it's mostly a slightly more expensive long distance bus, with all ages, dressed in the most casual imaginable clothing, and as likely to be visiting a friend as meeting a client. (My favorite example appeared in a *Wall Street Journal* story, depicting how a passenger attempted to pay for his drink using food stamps.)

Your buyers of yesterday (for example, vice president of sales and marketing) have evolved into today's leaner, electronic, empowered organization (for example, manager of the customer response center). Tomorrow, that buyer may be joined or replaced by a radically different one (for example, chief of customer interaction and satisfaction). When I began providing strategic consulting services, GTE was as high tech as it got; today, my clients include dotcoms all over the country whose products range from the unique to the incomprehensible. (But they're all well funded!)

Your brand(s) should have the widest possible appeal so that buyers you never even dreamed of can reasonably evaluate your potential for their situations. Don't specialize in sales for financial services or, worse, sales for telemarketers in financial services. Build your brand around sales. You can always narrow it down later in the conversation, but the idea is to obtain the conversation in the first place.

*Key: Cast a wide net, not a single hook.*

---

I'm constantly surprised at how stupid I was two weeks ago. And even that changes, because it used to be two months ago.

## Myth #6: Advertising Is the Be All and End All in Branding

Most advertising—in any form—is nearly worthless, because it tends to focus incorrectly on what you do rather than on what the buyer receives. It is task and input oriented rather than result and output oriented. I don't know about you, but I neither get in my car to drive past billboards, nor surf the net to find electronic billboards (AKA: websites).

A feature article in a major publication, an interview in a trade association newsletter, and/or a performance aid that companies eagerly apply are just some examples of brand alternatives that are superior to advertising. Especially in consulting, ads pale in comparison to referral, reference, and renown. Anyone can blow his or her own horn, but it's even more effective to have someone else playing your music.

While "public relations and advertising" was once the mantra, a strong case exists today for public relations alone, or at least in a superior position. Consultants interested in branding must "influence the influencers," meaning that it's often far more effective—exponential, in fact—to pursue editors, reporters, pundits, interviewers, alliance partners, trade association heads, allied professionals (attorneys or CPAs), who in turn influence your potential buyers.

A more direct influencer is outstanding service. My service standard is to return every single phone call within ninety minutes during normal working hours, and I hit this level of responsiveness 99 percent of the time. Clients and prospects alike talk about this, and it's become a part of my brand: "He's the most responsive consultant I've ever dealt with."

This means that, if you have staff, every single person is as responsible for the integrity of the brand as you are. If you don't have staff, all of your customer interactions will polish or tarnish the brand.

Don't rely on advertising alone. It can be an effective supplement. But your actions will speak louder for your brand than advertising ever will.

*Key: Advertise to support, not create, other brand initiatives.*

---

Advertising is best applied to products that are tangible and can be seen on a daily basis. If you do utilize advertising, use it to stress *results* and not what you do.

## Myth #7: You Can Only Brand a Tangible Product

Historically, most of the great brands have been product brands: Coke, Ford, Tide, Kleenex, and IBM. But that's because, historically, we were a product, manufacturing, and commodity economy. (The product emphasis became so great that, when I was young, there were a dozen or so cars to recognize: Ford, Chevy, Chrysler, etc. But by the time I was in college, there were hundreds of car "brands": [Buick] Rivera, [Chevy] Impala, [Nash] Rambler, and so on.)

Today, of course, we enjoy a knowledge economy. Whereas our main industrial drivers were once rubber, textiles, steel, and agriculture, there are today high tech, pharmaceuticals, communications, and so forth. According to sources, such as the American Society for Training and Development in training and Kennedy Information in consulting, the combined budgets spent on training, consulting, and related external learning and development is in excess of $200 billion annually *in the United States alone.* And these are conservative figures, because there are over 400,000 independent consultants, speakers, and trainers in the U.S. who are poorly represented in those figures.

Add to the knowledge economy the accelerated speed of change, and it becomes unwieldy to attempt to brand a product whose life cycle begins to resemble that of a may fly. Computers, phone systems, calculators, VCRs, stereos, and a myriad of other consumer products change almost daily. Consequently, the idea of branding an idea that was perpetuated throughout changing products became fashionable: Apple's "think different," Mercedes' "engineered like no other car in the world." (This form of branding was achieved decades ago when GE adopted the line "progress is our most important product," since it was manufacturing everything from light bulbs and washing machines to jet engines and locomotives.

In consulting, it's pragmatic and sensible to brand your ideas and approaches, since they may well be vested at different times in various products, services, expertise, approaches, methodologies, and so on. Think about branding ideas that are not reliant on a workshop delivery method, a rigid six-step template, or a clever matrix. Moreover, consider the ultimate transcendental brand, which has the most enduring nature of all in changing times: You.

*Key: The ultimate brand is your name, so long as its owner changes with the times.*

> The knowledge economy, global competition, rapid change, and
> short attention span of the buying public all require that your brand
> be affixed to ideas and approaches that don't age with the times.
> The best vacuum tube brand disappeared as fast as the most ineffec-
> tive vacuum tube brand.

## Myth #8: Brands Require Active, Aggressive Management

The whole point of my "gravitational field" earlier in this book is that you can put into place a variety of elements that will serve to continually attract people to you. Combined with effective brand recognition, those elements vary from zero maintenance (passive listings, product sales), to occasional tweaking (new position papers, periodic networking), to active engagement (speaking, pro bono work).

However, on any of these configurations, the brand is, in effect, "managing itself." You need spend only a minimal time on it and you certainly don't need a brand manager. (In fact, most consultants, no matter what size their practice or their firm, waste money on marketing people, who seldom develop even the business necessary to justify their own expense.)

How did IBM and AT&T survive terrible CEOs before finally finding the correct leadership for the times? Perhaps more dramatically, how did Apple survive the three consecutive disastrous tenures of CEOs before Steve Jobs returned to revitalize the place, particularly with Apple's far fewer resources at the time? It was able to do so because Apple had a rabid customer base in love with its "rebellious" brand and fascinated by the technology. Without those customers who stayed loyal through such inept product development, distribution, and service, the company would have surely collapsed of its own incompetence.

Although you're reading a book on branding, you shouldn't have to spend a lot of time on branding once your essential elements are in place. The only exception would occur if and when you choose to create additional brands, which would entail incorporating them correctly into your "gravity."

Your focus must be on the acquisition and delivery of business. Branding is a marketing device to turbocharge those efforts, a means to those ends. It is not and should not be a separate end requiring high levels of attention and investment.

*Key: A brand should be agile, not ponderous and requiring heavy lifting.*

---

The success of the brand is measured solely by the growth of your profits. "Intel inside" is a clever conceptual brand, which creates high sales. Edsel was a highly clear tangible brand that was heavily promoted and failed dismally—and has come to represent abject brand failure. Highly recognized brands that don't sell are worthless.

## Myth #9: Brands Need to Be Specific and Focused

Gillette once made razors and razor blades when King Gillette founded the company. And while the organization still does so, it also produces an assortment of toiletries, from shaving cream to deodorant. In fact, a learned marketing professor once intoned loftily to my class that one had to see Gillette as a market-driven company, exclusively in men's toiletries. Yet today the company provides women's products as well.

*Playboy* magazine has consistently used its brand name to explore ventures into other publishing products, cable television, videos, clothing, jewelry, and additional items. Both Hewlett-Packard and IBM have used their brands to embrace large-scale moves into business consulting (now a major part of IBM's profit).

The ultimate brand is *you*. If your name carries enough celebrity and impact (Peter Drucker, Tom Peters, Michael Hammer, to name a few of "guru-level" fame), it will provide an umbrella for virtually any undertaking. But even short of that celebrity, your brand can have broad appeal in an industry (telecommunications), for a methodology (strategy), for a condition (turn-around expertise), for a specialty (expert witness), or for a geography (the finest consultant in New England).

The good news is that you can establish the segment, slice, or situation which makes the most sense for your branding efforts. The bad news is that this relatively high state of ambiguity causes many people to become frustrated with the branding process.

My advice is to attempt to create the brands with the broadest possible appeal for your expertise and your passion, while still creating a "perimeter" within which to focus (such as the categories above). It's overly narrow to brand the "Acme Consulting six-step sales acceleration process." It's much more flexible, more enduring, and more appealing to be known as "The Influencer."

*Key: Choose your own brand playing field before developing your playbook.*

---

This is a conceptual, abstract economy, with words like "virtual" and "cyberspace" filling the ether. Brands should be more about communicating and ideal than labeling a box.

## Myth #10: Brands Must Continually Grow Toward Universal Recognition

If you define your market as the universal consumer, then universal recognition is, indeed, mandatory. It would be unthinkable for McDonald's or Coca-Cola or American Airlines to seek anything less than brand appreciation in all global areas in which they operate or seek to operate.

But that's not really a consultant's world.

What's important for consultants is to achieve brand recognition *in those market segments that are important for current and future business.* If your strategy is to travel only minimally and become known as the finest strategy consultant in the southeast, it's important that potential buyers in Atlanta and Miami recognize your brand, but not necessarily those in Los Angeles and Denver. If your market is executive coaching for small business owners, your brand does not have to reach Fortune 1000 management. If you specialize in continuous flow processes, your brand is better aimed at operations managers than at human resource people.

Your brand efforts should be circumscribed by your marketplace. (Which is why it's almost always silly to appear in a media event that your potential buyers don't watch or listen to.) Bigger isn't always better, and focus often outweighs size. I too often hear customers say to consultants, "Why are you such a well-kept secret?" If those customers are outside of your market segments, that's perfectly acceptable; if they are a part of your market segment, that is death.

Branding may be as localized as you wish, even though it has broad potential. The important test is whether you are saturating the markets you've identified with your brand. Too many brands are widely known by people who are not potential customers, and virtually unknown by those who are!

*Key: It's usually more important to hone your brand than to grow your brand.*

---

There is a local restaurant with lines out the door every morning, known simply as "the best breakfast in town." That's a great example of very localized, highly effective branding. It doesn't help if they know that in the next state, but it's important that they know it down the block.

## Myth #11: The Brand Is External to the Customer

Earlier I referred to Erhard Seminar Training that consisted of a rather rigorous weekend "training" session during which the trainers often berated the audience for their own weaknesses. It attracted a cult following in an era of "new age" approaches and made a temporary fortune for its creator, Werner Erhard.[2]

Est was run and administered by a volunteer, cult-like, and rabid core of former participants who proselytized, cajoled, and even intimidated prospective participants. No one would describe the experience for consideration beforehand. "You had to experience it to 'get' it." Est had marvelously incorporated its own "customers" into its branding campaign.

Word of mouth is one of the greatest examples of customer involvement with the brand's proliferation, and one of the most effective. When a buyer says

---

[2]He claimed to receive the basis for est during an epiphany while driving across the Golden Gate Bridge.

to another buyer, "You need Alan Weiss for this project, trust me, he's done wonders for us," you don't need much more other than to cash the check. I estimate that upwards of 80 percent of my product sales and newsletter subscriptions originate through personal referrals.

It's important to *allow* your customers to participate in the brand. This can be as crude as free T-shirts with your logo for participants, or as delicate and sophisticated as highly focused testimonials with attribution. Business doesn't exist without clients, and neither do brands. The greatest acceleration you can provide is to allow your clients to participate.

As you work with your clients and move toward completion of projects, develop plans to incorporate your customer and your results into your brand. These actions may include:

- Testimonials for your marketing materials that emphasize the brand (for example, "The 'Team Builder' didn't just help our team, she moved our team to an entirely new level of effectiveness").
- Add the client credibility to your brand: "These clients are among those organizations which have profited from the 'Team Builder': . . . ."
- Provide plastic cards, charts, book marks, paperweights, and other office adornments that promote your brand, since you have a multitude of potential new clients within existing clients.
- Send a newsletter or other communication regularly to all past participants, or buyers, or implementers, or people you've met in the client organization that emphasizes your brand: "The Team Builder Newsletter" or "Team Builder Techniques of the Month."

*Key: Embrace the customer in the brand; don't hog it for yourself.*

---

Clients can quickly become zealous brand publicity sources. When I use a word such as "organic" in a client organization to emphasize flexibility, I find that the word enters the client lexicon within twenty-four hours, and I find it continually flung back at me. The same applies to brands. "We need the Team Builder in the field force."

## Myth #12: Brands in and of Themselves Have Little Value Without Substance

I'm not advocating "brand without substance" by a long shot, but I do want to suggest that certain branding efforts develop an intrinsic value of their own. Customer "good will" is more than an abstract concept; it's a valuable asset. So is a respected brand.

I'm often asked by solo practitioners if they will be able to sell their business some day, and how their practice can be objectively valuated. While I never had any intention of perpetuating my own firm beyond my lifetime and have never had even a single employee, I have also learned that several of my brands have acquired an inherent value, which may make purchase by someone (I would expect from my estate) of interest.

Consider the "McNally" series of books written by Lawrence Sanders.

## VIGNETTE

Near the end of Frank Sinatra's career, his concerts continued to sell out, despite his occasionally erratic voice and an increasing tendency to forget the lyrics to his own songs. (There were always strategically placed teleprompters around the room, and I once nearly fell through a monitor flush with the stage floor when I spoke at a venue the night prior to Mr. Sinatra's performance.)

Fans weren't attending to hear the quality of his voice, or his ability to remember every lyric. They were going to be a part of the Sinatra brand, the *zeitgeist,* which had comforted them for most of their adult lives.

Why are there people in the seats for Chicago Cubs games or for an "oldies" group that has now seen the other side of sixty, or in line at a restaurant that features mediocre food served after a two-hour wait? Because the brand has long since superceded the quality of the product.

I'm not advocating that you allow yourself to decline or put your clients at an inconvenience. But strong brand attraction can withstand mistakes, errors, and even poor quality, at least for a while. In other words, it wins you the "benefit of the doubt" every time.

They were highly regarded detective stories and hugely successful commercially. Unfortunately, after scores of books and at a ripe old age, Mr. Sanders passed away. However, the family did an interesting thing. Recognizing the power of the "McNally brand" (as apart from Mr. Sanders as a brand), they commissioned a fine writer (Vincent Lardo) to continue the series, which he has to widespread praise. This is a vivid example of a brand *intimately associated with its creator* being perpetuated beyond the creator's lifetime.

There is every reason to believe that such a transition can be achieved by consultants—and that they don't have to die to pull it off. If your brands are sufficiently recognized within given marketplaces, if your expertise is transferable, and if your methodologies are adaptable by others, your brand(s) (for better or for worse) may just be strong enough to transcend your departure.

Earlier, I advocated that the ultimate brand is your name, and I fervently believe that to be true, because it can't be appropriated by others and can readily change with the times. However, I've also shown that author Tom Clancy has "loaned" his brand to books actually written by others. At the beginning or end of virtually every major motion picture, we see a line that says, "A Penny Marshall film," which means that the director is creating his or her brand embracing that film, even though it may have been written, produced, and acted by others.

As you develop your brands, it's never too early to consider what may be necessary to perpetuate them beyond your own association with them, thereby creating equity in the brands themselves. Perhaps solo practitioners don't sell their firms—they sell their brands.

*Key: View a brand as a corporate asset, not merely a marketing device.*

---

I was once reluctant to see my name all over everything, since I prided myself on client results. I've learned, however, that the two are not mutually exclusive. After all, my publishers place my name in large print in their books, so why shouldn't I highlight it in my materials? We're proud of saying, "My word is my bond." Well, perhaps our name is also our brand, and our brand is our long-term equity.

# BRAND NEW LESSONS

Branding has been with us forever, but as it's been recognized as a valuable technique in the information age it has attracted self-styled experts and pundits. It's important to recognize the valid supports of branding and to discard the invalid suppositions and mythology.

Here are the twelve myths stated as positives:

**Fact #1:** An appeal to emotions, not logic, will achieve action

**Fact #2:** You should create need, not merely react to "wants"

**Fact #3:** Substance and pragmatics are more important than catch phrases

**Fact #4:** You can develop a brand tomorrow and achieve recognition rapidly

**Fact #5:** Effective brands in consulting are about ideas, not about specific products

**Fact #6:** Advertising is only a minor brand enhancement

**Fact #7:** You can readily brand services, ideas, and concepts

**Fact #8:** Brands can be effective with relatively little aggressive management

**Fact #9:** Brands can be general and widely embracing

**Fact #10:** Brands require recognition only in your ideal market segments

**Fact #11:** The best brands include and embrace the client

**Fact #12:** A brand in and of itself may represent equity and inherent value

# CHAPTER 7

# Publicizing Your Brand Within Your "Environment"

*Expanding Fifteen Minutes of Fame into a Month of Sundays*

A friend of mine, Patricia Fripp, is a very successful professional speaker. Her brand, publicly, is "A speaker for all reasons." She candidly calls herself, privately, "a shameless self-promoter." The only problem with the latter phrase is that it's redundant.

Whether our brand is larger than life, or low key and subtle, we have to publicize and promote it to the world of our potential buyers. But that final phrase is the key range finder: "potential buyers." We don't just shoot our artillery into the sky, but aim it at the target. The primary target is potential buyers, and the secondary target is recommenders to those buyers.

Thus, before we can be successful at any kind of brand promotion, we have to have answered the three questions raised earlier in this book and this series:

1. What is the specific value added you bring to a client, in terms of improved business outcomes?
2. Who, specifically, can write a check for that value?
3. How do I reach those people?

This is a process I call "thinking from the outside in," meaning that you are concerned with your end user, customer, and buyer, not with your features, benefits, and traditional strengths. Conventional salespeople and sales tactics approached the buyer from a position of emphasizing features and benefits. Contemporary and future consultative salespeople and tactics call for understanding (or identifying) the buyer's needs and demonstrating how those needs will be met as you organize your services around those needs.

There is no more "one size fits all," which is why Mercedes can market an inexpensive urban model while also introducing a new six-figure "Maybach," which will compete with Rolls-Royce at the very top end. McDonald's features fast-food burgers and fries as well as healthier salads. Delta and US Airways offer both one-class, inexpensive shuttles and traditional first-class accommodations. Comprehensive consulting practices offer both systemic, organization design assistance and individual executive coaching.

> Brand support is less about our strengths and self-recognized abilities than it is about buyer needs and the buyer's perception of our abilities to meet those needs.

## UNDERSTANDING THE BRAND ENVIRONMENT

So, our brands have to be more than merely effective representations of who we are and what we do. They must also be "buyer-friendly." That means that your buyers have been accurately identified at the outset, and you're continually monitoring the environment for evolution and/or new buyers. That evolution is important, because we often misconstrue why buyers are buying.

The reason New Coke was such a fiasco is that Coca-Cola presumed that buyers were making intellectual decisions about the company's product, not emotional ones. (Yet it's emotion, not logic, that makes people act.) In blind taste tests meticulously conducted by Coca-Cola and its consultants, consumers reported that what was to be New Coke was a very fine drink. The test reports showed a highly favorable rating by Coke drinkers.

The problem was that Coke never mentioned to the test subjects that New Coke was to *replace* the existing product. The emotional loss of the old standby created a case-study consumer reaction that forced the company to reverse its decision. Yet, in subsequent blind taste tests, even the most vociferous supporters of the original Coke couldn't readily tell it apart from New Coke. This was not an objective issue of product quality, but a subjective and emotional issue of product loyalty.

These combinations of consumer reaction, perception, the company's positioning of its brands, competitive actions (7UP took out ads during this fiasco saying, "Never changed, never will"), and other factors constitute a brand "environment." The environment can be influenced by your decisions and choices, but it can't be absolutely controlled and, therefore, can never be ignored.

For consulting services, the traditional branding, such as it was, was rationally based on something like this:

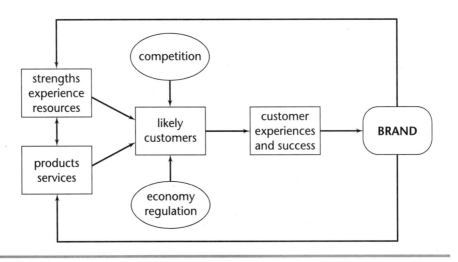

**Figure 7.1.** Traditional Branding Environment

In the traditional branding environment, the consulting firm began with its own strengths, methodology, and expertise, and the products and services that were the product of or the fuel underlying those resources. For example, a strategy firm might have expertise in identifying driving forces, creating missions and vision, competitive market analysis, and competitive intelligence. The products and services may have been strategy retreats, board-level interviews and analyses, industry reports, and competitive intelligence assignments.

The likely customers may have been owners of small firms and CEOs of larger firms. However, the competition was an uncontrolled factor (McKinsey has had a brand name in strategy and Boston Consulting Group has had its famous double axis matrix of "star," "dog," and so on), as was the economy. The competition could introduce a technology, approach, or best-selling book, which made the consulting firm's approach passé or simplistic in the eyes of buyers, and the economy might have made strategy "unimportant" (everyone is doing so well), or "unaffordable" (everyone is losing money and can't afford the help).

> Branding never takes place in a vacuum. It occurs in an environment that can be influenced and even partially controlled. You have to thoroughly understand your brand's environment or it might be inappropriately dressed, prepared, and depicted.

Where the consulting firm is successful, its customers represent a strong influence or even control of the brand identity. "If these are the people with whom we've been successful, avoiding both the competitive threats and utilizing the current economy well, then we must orient our future efforts around that sequence." In other words, if you've successfully run the gauntlet, then let's replicate the process. In this case, the brand is formed from past success and then serves to complete the loop by influencing the promotion and future products and services and the orientation and allocation of resources.

Frankly, I don't believe that such linear and sequential thinking works any more. The reasons are these:

- In an electronic, high-tech world, influence can be rapid and change by customer or conditions.
- In a global economy, our buyers and their needs frequently shift.

- The model is based more on a traditional product mentality than on a service economy reality.
- Brands can't be formed primarily from experience, or we'll be forever two steps behind the times and sadly in arrears of the future. They must be formed in preparation for the future, anticipating conditions.
- Brands should not be formulated based on current strengths or historical successes, but rather on future buyer need. This model works from the "inside out," not the "outside in."

## CREATING THE NEW ENVIRONMENT

The consulting world in which we'll all be working is one of increasing interdependence and complexity. It is based on need, not deliverables, on relationships, not products, and on results, not tasks. The branding process and its promotion will take place within a much more interactive and non-linear sequence.

In Figure 7.2 I've chosen to depict *just a small sample* of the interactions that can shape your brand. The brand isn't a beginning or an ending point, but rather an integral aspect of your business.

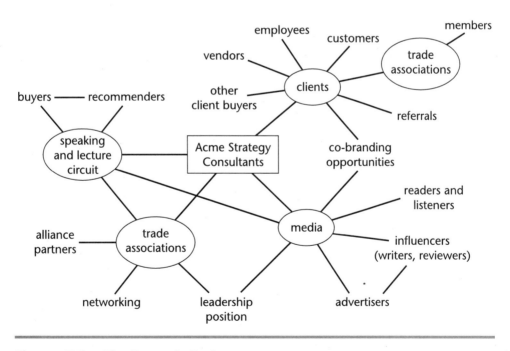

**Figure 7.2.** The Dynamic Environment

In a complex world, influence at one point will result in change at another, distant point. Brand influence, therefore, is exponential and dynamic, with relatively little effort creating great movement.

Bear in mind that the figure simply includes one client for our fictional Acme Consulting. Assuming that Acme would probably have a dozen current clients and scores of former clients, you can see how complex and huge the chart and the interactions can become. In that complexity is its simplicity.

The publicizing of the brand must take place in this dynamic context. For example, if your prospective buyer needs are anticipated as being "strategy for utilizing technology to market globally," then your brand "The Global Marketer" should be the one that you speak about on the lecture circuit, directly to buyers and recommenders. It should be on prominent display in your work in trade associations, so that your networking can lead you to prospective clients and/or alliance partners (for example, a similar firm working exclusively in Europe, encouraging work in the U.S.). Your media interviews and articles must feature this approach, appealing to those who can influence still others.

However, let's assume that you anticipate more changes in the environment, and that within your core competency of strategic change the embrace of diversity becomes an important need for future buyers. You don't have to revamp your products and services, and you needn't try to calculate competitive actions. You simply begin to adjust your matrix influence by changing the nature of your articles, interviews, speaking, networking, and so on.

If you view the matrix holistically, you'll find that you can create change—brand publicity and its direction—by intervening at various points in an intelligent and very low cost manner. And note that the matrix does, indeed, go off the page. The trade associations that your clients belong to, for example, are excellent marketing and publicity opportunities, which have their own members, their own networking, their own media contacts, etc.

This non-sequential or matrix view of brand publicity will be different for

A friend of mine has a pacemaker installed to regulate her heartbeat.

Not long ago, she decided to network by attending a session in Chicago comprising consultants and speakers, and she figured the expense would be well worth it for the expansion of her influence and contacts.

On the way to the hotel meeting room the first morning, she saw a sign advising of a meeting for the manufacturers of her pacemaker. She impulsively burst into the room during their meeting and, all eyes on her, explained that she wanted to thank them for saving her life. The participants urged her to stay and say a few words to the full group, which she did extemporaneously.

She arrived at her networking meeting late, but related this story (which is how I heard it, as I was running the meeting). A week later, she received a request to do some work for the pacemaker company, which she eagerly accepted at a higher rate of pay than she had ever earned before.

Is this serendipity? Is it simply moxie and assertiveness? Perhaps. But it's also a fine example of the new branding environment and of the interrelationships that are created every day through electronic media, word of mouth, networking, and combinations thereof.

---

every firm, given its specialty, focus, and client base. It's really another way of using the gravitational elements and reorganizing them around their interactions with current and former clients. The important consideration is to create this matrix for your firm, whether sole practitioner or larger operation, and create plans for how you intend to promote and publicize your brand within and among the interrelationships.

If you'd like a less visual and more methodical approach, you can create worksheets around the same concept. Here are examples for some of the categories:

Current Clients:
- buyers
- recommenders

|  | • potential buyers |
|  | • their trade association membership |
|  | • their venders |
| Former Clients: | • prior buyers |
|  | • potential new buyers |
|  | • recommenders |
|  | • their trade association membership |
|  | • their venders |
| Media: | • editors |
|  | • reporters and interviewers |
|  | • other advertisers |
| Your Trade Association(s): | • other members as alliance partners |
|  | • networking |
|  | • leadership position visibility |
|  | • media connections |

Publicizing your brand means promoting it within your particular environment, which is more complex, far-reaching, and high-impact than you think. This is why it's useful to actually map the interactions.

## TEN GUIDELINES FOR INFLUENCING THE ENVIRONMENT

There are some systematic approaches to ensure that the necessary complexity doesn't become frustrating ambiguity.

1. *Physically chart your environment.* Take an easel sheet or white board that you don't otherwise need, and map out all of the various influence targets and interactions. Don't try to do it on the computer, because you'll be limited by the screen and you won't be able to see everything readily. Let yourself go crazy. Include every conceivable influence on your brand, and those you wish to influence with your brand.

2. *Establish priorities.* Not every element or interaction will be equally important. A client whose project was completed ten years ago will likely not be as important as a current client. A website (which is passive) may not be nearly as important as a monthly electronic newsletter (which is active). Some media sources hold much more potential than others. Use different colors to create a triage effect: (a) absolutely critical for brand promotion; (b) important interactions and further connections; (c) minor help with for further matrix connections.

3. *Review this at least monthly.* Your condition will constantly change. Include new, major elements and eliminate unpromising ones and dead ends (for example, one of your clients doesn't belong to any relevant trade associations). Highlight those connections and interactions that have been most successful, and look for patterns (for example, we have a story to tell which the print media loves but hasn't translated well into our public speaking activities).

4. *Create the most comprehensive brand publicity approach you can.* You might choose those avenues which have maximum "interlocks with others" to heighten your effect. Or you might focus on connections with the greatest numbers of buyers. However, you may want to consider a branding publicity approach that blankets your entire environmental "countryside." Once you have things charted, you should be able to develop effective approaches. The must: Ensure that your priority elements are hit hardest.

5. *Build brand strategy and publicity into alliances and affiliations.* If you're sponsoring an event at a trade association, cite it in the program and on the stage as funded by "The Team Builder," or whatever your brand is. If you are participating in a joint seminar series with a marketing partner, the print material might read, "Featuring the Consultant's Consultant: Alan Weiss." If you and your partner both have websites with hyperlinks to each other, label your link on the other site with "click here to visit The Strategist."

6. *Apprise your marketing and publicity people to be consistent.* You may be employing, at least situationally, graphic designers, publicity people, advertising agencies, and similar venders or subcontractors. Educate them about your brand and your environmental strategy. Make sure they are consistent and that they exploit their opportunities. For example, a new brochure or a directory listing should prominently feature the brand identification.

Your environment will often surprise you once you formally chart it. You'll find you have more "reach" and scope than you imagined, and that you're currently attempting to influence only a small portion of it.

7. *Place the brand in your email signature file.* Few elements will reach your entire environmental complex as well or as frequently as your email. It's a simple matter to include the brand as a statement in your signature files. Keep these short, and in plain text, since most software in these programs still won't accurately translate bold characters, colors, graphics, etc. You can, of course, include the brand in a fancier manner on your letterhead, business cards, and envelopes.

8. *Work the brand into every single interview and article.* When a reporter asks, "Is your approach to productivity based on first building effective teams?" respond, "Yes, and that's why I'm known as The Team Builder, because my approaches create teams faster and with more cohesion than any other. . . ." Print column inches and broadcast sound bites are both squeezed for time, and catchy phrases and labels are usually welcome.

9. *Direct everyone to "brand central."* There will be some areas in which you can truly expand on and promote your brand far better than others. You can't do much in a signature file, but you can do a lot in a position paper. However, one of the absolute best places is your website, which can contain color, graphics, testimonials, free articles—even audio and video. As with your print brochure and press kit, this is an area that can blatantly promote the brand. Therefore, you should direct people to these "brand central" locations. Put your website on all your materials, email, stationery, etc. (My unscientific survey reveals that over 75 percent of all print ads contain a website reference today.) Don't merely send an article to someone, but send it in your press kit with your brand emphasis.

10. Test the brand's reach and impact regularly. Access various parts of your environmental map and determine how and when people there would come into contact with your brand under present conditions and with

your current plans in place. Ask people what they've heard and what they perceive about the brand. It's one thing to spread the brand, but it's another to ensure that the right people are deriving the right message from it.

I once worked for a consulting firm by the name of Kepner-Tregoe, founded in the late 1950s by Chuck Kepner and Ben Tregoe. The firm specialized in decision making, problem solving, and strategy, very pragmatic and essential skills. Eventually, Ben owned the company himself and was always proud of the name as the brand, even though people had trouble pronouncing it (many clients called us "Captain Trigger") and it was far from memorable.

Ben changed his mind one day when he met a man in a hotel bar who, learning of Ben's identity, said, "You folks are that training company. I'd recognize the name anywhere. You provided the most valuable technique I've ever used in the ten years since I took your courses."

"And what was that?" Ben asked proudly.

Whipping out a yellow highlighter from an inside pocket, the man said, "I had never used one of these before, and it was great for marking all that dry, boring material you gave me. I've bought them direct from the manufacturer ever since."

---

> The great thing about publicizing your brand is that there is no one special way to do it. The horrible thing about publicizing your brand is that there is no one special way to do it.

## TWENTY-FIVE WAYS TO FOSTER PUBLICITY IN ANY ENVIRONMENT

No matter what your environment, there are some ideas that may work immediately and effectively for you. Here is a buffet. There's no need to try to put everything on your plate at once, since you can always return. If some food disagrees with you, then move to the next station. But no one I've ever seen leaves a buffet line with an empty plate.

*1. Build a Spear Point, Not a Bludgeon.*   The more adjectives and descriptors you use in your brand, the more generalized you risk it becoming. (That's why your name, alone, might be the ultimate brand.) "Kodak moments" was a nice brand touch, and far superior to "special photographic moments captured for all time with the use of Kodak 400-speed film." Keep honing your brand. Penetration is inversely proportional to breadth.

*2. Establish Clear Targets.*   People don't jump and cheer when you hit the target (especially if it's the side of a barn) but do become enthusiastic when you hit the bull's eye. Despite your more generalized branding scope, there are some targets on your map that are far more valuable than others. Aim your strongest, most focused efforts there, for example, to the vice presidents of sales of major consumer products organizations, not merely to senior managers across all large industries.

*3. Get There Firstest with the Mostest.*   Confederate General Nathan Bedford Forrest really didn't say that (it was more like, "I arrive before the enemy with superior forces"), but the point is nonetheless well-taken. If you're first, you'll get better publicity. I've long held a brand as the "contrarian," because I'll take an opposite view to prevailing wisdom (for example, "Why quality control measures produce poorer quality"). Don't follow someone else's niche, but establish your own to be the first one there. Don't take on the 5,000-pound gorilla.

*4. Never Rest.*   As the brand grows and is accepted, you can't allow it to "coast." I once thought that all film came in yellow boxes because Kodak did. A separate set of actions is often necessary to support high-flying brands. In consulting, for example, it's useful to publish regularly with your brand's prominent mention, to keep it in the eye of the potential buyer. Andersen Consulting, before the split with Andersen, engaged in a great deal of promotion to perpetuate the brand.

*5. Establish Visceral Uniqueness.*   People say "FedEx" it, or "hand me a Band-Aid," or "I'd like a Formica countertop." When your brand becomes synonymous with an emotional need, you've scored a home run. Many a CEO, needing strategy help, has simply said to a subordinate, "Get McKinsey," just as purchasing managers have "IBM" on their Rolodex (another fine example, Rolodex), under "computers."

There is always the threat of a brand becoming generic in the buyer's mind, like Kleenex, Formica, or Band-Aid. But that's a small risk to take when you are associated with the ultimate service in your field. Find the niches that allow you to do that with the greatest ease.

*6. Might Makes Right.* Establish leadership credentials and authority. When people ask for "The Telephone Doctor," they get Nancy Friedman, and not one hundred other consultants who provide help with the phone. Good tag lines for any brand are "The leader in . . .," "The most respected . . .," "The most widely cited . . .," and so on. Speak in prestigious environments, publish in respected publications, network at important events, take leadership positions in visible industry associations. Demonstrate your impeccable credentials in your brand area.

*7. Don't Overemphasize Quality.* Hear me out. No one *needs* a Ferrari. People buy them because of the allure, status, and mystery (trust me), but not because they need transportation. Montblanc pens knocked Cross pens out of the luxury status box *not* through superior writing mechanics, but through superior marketing (fat pens, luxury appearance, snooty ads). As I heard a woman speaker state candidly from the stage, "I wear two watches all the time. The Timex is so that I can see it. The Rolex is so you can see it." Brands thrive on emotion, not logic.

*8. Control the Message.* The legendary genius who instantly doubled his company's consumer product sales with zero investment simply made this suggestion: "On the directions for our shampoo, let's include the phrase 'rinse and repeat.'" That phrase doubled usage in one stroke. Manage perception. An example: "Ask your direct reports to cite your strategy in thirty seconds. If you don't hear the same message from each one, call The Strategist immediately. If you hear conflicting messages, try to make an appointment this afternoon." Should this strategy recitation be expected and important? Apparently so. . . .

***9. Get Real.*** Buyers must be able to recognize you. That Kepner-Tregoe name was a problem. Toyota thought that the Lexus must be isolated from the parent company if buyers were to take the new luxury brand seriously. To this day, the Japanese high-performance sports car, Accura NSX, doesn't sell well. Why? Because serious sports car buyers want Italian or German machines (or at the lower end, a Corvette). Establish an easy and relevant identity. "The Questor System for Sales" means absolutely nothing to me or any buyer. "The Sales Accelerator" is more to the point and descriptive.

***10. Create an Umbrella, Not a Stretcher.*** You may have a brand that says "Quality Decisions," which includes application to hiring, evaluations, acquisitions, customer service, and so on. It's better to have those separate services under your umbrella, as an embrace or cover, than to have "Quality Decisions in Hiring," "Quality Decisions in Evaluations," and so on. You can stretch a brand too far through constant labeling—and attenuate its effectiveness. Unlike cattle, there's no need to brand every individual steer.

***11. Welcome the Competition.*** Burger King builds restaurants across from McDonald's because they know that people go there to buy hamburgers. Competition broadens markets; it doesn't restrict them. The key is to stand out in the crowd. I've used "million dollar consultant" to distinguish me from legions of other consultants, and I've described my practice as "boutique" for those buyers meriting personalized attention (after I educate them about the need for such individualized attention!). I don't mind the hall being filled—I just want the spotlight on me.

> Never bad mouth or bemoan the competition. Welcome it as a true indicator of market need. Then strive to make yourself stand out in that crowd. It's best to be a strange number 1 than a run-of-the-mill, vanilla 64th.

***12. Be Your Own Promoter.*** You control the bold type, italic type, and colors on your materials. Set yourself apart physically and emotionally. It's better to be a strange number 1 than a run-of-the-mill, vanilla number 64. When a local barber was threatened by a new chain beauty salon across the street advertising $6 haircuts, he put up a sign immediately that said, "We fix $6 haircuts." What are you doing to demonstrate to people the true uniqueness you feel about yourself and your approaches? If you can't shamelessly self-promote yourself, then who will?

*13. Understand Which Is Tail, Which Is Dog.* Your firm is designed, one supposes, to create income for you and your family and to support certain lifestyles. Brands are a tool in your company's toolkit, along with financing, equipment, employees, and so on. Your firm is a means to an end, which is your life; and your brand is a means to an end, which is your company. Don't become

## VIGNETTE

A successful but "stuck" consultant named Rick asked me for advice to improve revenues. He was successfully attracting clients such as Coca-Cola and McDonald's, but he wasn't making enough money nor leveraging what he was doing.

"Let's start with your value," I said. "How would you define it?"

"It's my cassettes," he said, to my utter astonishment, proudly holding up an album of ten audiotapes and a workbook.

"But that's only you on tape," I stuttered. "Your real value is the ability to build the client's revenues and market share without capital investment through smarter selling."

"No, I use my consulting and speaking opportunities to sell these tapes. They sell for an average of $99 per album, and I try to move several hundred through the sales force."

It took me three months to convince him that he could easily charge $250,000 for his sales consulting work, and give away the cassettes for free in the bargain. It was an absolute shock to his value system.

We often allow the tail to wag the dog. We need to put more weight on the dog.

obsessed with your brand(s)—you can alter, discard, improve, and replace brands with impunity, provided your company is better off for the changes. Never forget which is the fuel for the other.

*14. Sub-Brands Are Too Often Substandard.*   Although Mercedes managed to be effective in both the top and bottom ends of the market, Calvin Klein undermined it's fine name with a series of disastrous brand extensions to low-priced stores. When Marriott purchased Ritz-Carlton, it did not name the hotels the "Ritz-Carlton Marriott." Keep your brand relatively lofty. There's no need to apply it to minor workshops, small reports, and unimportant efforts. "The Strategist" doesn't have to attach that brand to pro bono work at the corner gas station, which is owned by a friend.

*15. Egalitarianism Works for Multiple Brands.*   So long as your efforts are of equal weight and proportion, you can create co-equal brands with great effectiveness. Procter & Gamble has been the king of this realm, often creating competing brands to vie against each other on the same shelves (thereby leaving less room for brands from competing companies). "The Strategist," "The Team Builder," "The Facilitator," and "The Coach's Coach" might all exist, aimed at various parts of your brand environment. It might or might not make sense to list them all together, since it has the appearance of trying to be all things to all people. But why not take the concept and spread it among equal services aimed at different buyers?

*16. Visibility Requires, Well, Visuals.*   Logos always help. They don't have to be the most brilliant piece of art or graphics in the world, but they should be readily recognizable and promote your brand's identity. On one of my "best practices" book series published by Kennedy Information, we have a pair of hands on each cover, creating a proposal, writing a marketing plan, calculating fees, and so on. That particular brand logo creates a consistent and provocative image. Invest in a logo that is memorable for your buyer and directly leads that buyer to you.

*17. Save Your Money Elsewhere.*   Invest in your branding, both visually and textually. This is your leading edge. The only worse thing than no brand identity is a lousy brand identity (think "Edsel" or "Pinto" which, in Spanish, means "small penis"). Have your copy proofread and tested. Find the best graphic artists. Use seasoned web designers. Check thoroughly into trademark and service mark status. This is not the place to stint. Never use two-color graphics if you can use four-color.

**18. Don't Stop at the Borders.** On your environmental map, make sure that you include a global view. A brand should be trans-cultural to the maximum extent possible. Strategy is strategy, and teamwork is teamwork. In many respects, U.S. management practices travel far better than U.S. products, in that they are welcome overseas and have relatively little competition. As you develop your brands, try to make them universal so that you won't have to alter them later when you "get around to" international promotion.

**19. Patience Is Longer Than Tomorrow.** Although you can establish a brand virtually overnight in the electronic economy, it doesn't mean that you will or should. Your brand, especially if it's to be your name, might require lengthy development. You might develop some brands more quickly than others, for example, an approach might be faster ("Service Center Excellence") than your name, and for good reason. Prepare to make a longer-term investment and to take a longer-term focus. If you are diligent about the environment, marketing "gravity," and publicity, a year is an appropriate time frame to stimulate brand recognition.

**20. Additions Beat Alterations.** If you've established a brand, it's usually easier to add new brands than to artificially enlarge the old one. Kentucky Fried Chicken became KFC, but people still think of it as fried chicken, and not much else. Lexus did work when it was marketed as a new brand and not a Toyota extension. I'd have a hard time imagining Southwest Airlines as a luxury carrier, and people did have a tough time seeing United (through its shuttle service) as a low-cost carrier. Don't change your brands capriciously, not even to embrace other services. You're usually better served with new brands.

---

There's no way that McDonald's would ever appeal as an adult, superior restaurant. The adult-oriented "Arch Deluxe" burger was a disaster. They would have been better off creating a different restaurant experience altogether. (Apparently they are adding "sit-down appeal" in the form of adult meals at their current sites.)

**21. Use Triage Ruthlessly.**   Promote and exploit your successful brands, put investment into those that still have great potential and can springboard on the successful ones, and eliminate those that have gone nowhere or have outlived their relevance and impact. Don't maintain brands out of loyalty or emotion. They will detract from your more effective brands. If a consultant is still using "left brain/right brain" in his or her brands, it a sure sign of dating and lack of change with the times (the approach is pretty much thoroughly debunked). Reengineering is over, if you haven't heard. If a brand only affects a small portion of your environmental map, jettison it.

**22. Strive for Synonymy.**   Eventually, your brand should actually be the solution to the need. Michael Hammer *was* reengineering. Spencer Johnson and Ken Blanchard *were* "One Minute Management." Tom Peters *was* "The Search for Excellence." There were no options, except for hangers-on and emulators. "The Strategist for the Dotcom" is a beautiful answer to a particular market and solution. "The Team Builder for Volunteers" does the same thing. How closely can you be the perfect solution?

**23. Get Technical.**   There is an unquestioned cachet about technology and the Internet. No matter what your brand areas, create an attachment to technology so that there is a modern and innovative feel for your approach. A good website, hyperlinks on the web, fax on demand responses to questions, rapid telephone responsiveness, and other features of your interaction can provide a thoroughly modern appeal to whatever you do. If your brand is in teamwork, have a chat room available on your site for teams you're helping, accessible by password. You can brand the approach "The Virtual Team" or "The Electronic Team Room."

**24. Consider Anthropomorphism.**   Many organizations have used animals (Tony the Tiger or Charlie the Tuna) to represent them. There's nothing wrong with a little humor and self-effacing attitude. (Can you imagine a law firm branded with a shark motif?) Step outside purely business boundaries and consider other sources. I know a consultant who specializes in corporate and product naming and branding. His company has a logo of a path in the woods and the name "Appellation Trails." (It takes a minute!) I know another person, a woman, in the same business, who calls herself, "The Name Chick."

**25. Believe It.** Have some passion about your brand. Don't let it lie there like a stapler or a copy machine. Believe in what it represents, and don't be bashful about using it and promoting it. Remember, the first sale is always to yourself.

## BRAND NEW LESSONS

Brand publicity takes place in an environment that can identify and "map." That environment is dynamic. It is not linear or sequential, but interactive and organic. You should maximize the "coverage" of your map, using multiple brands as needed. Pursue those areas with the most payoff: The largest number of potential customers, the most media coverage, the maximum referrals, etc.

There are well over two dozen publicity devices to promote your brand. Choose a few and move them forward a mile; don't choose all of them and move an inch. You can always return for more.

# CHAPTER 8

# Creating Products to Boost Your Brand

## *The Wonderful Combination of Passive Income and Active Promotion*

Originally, brands pertained to and supported products. Brand management is still common in organizations as diverse as consumer giant Procter & Gamble and pharmaceutical leader Merck & Co. Many times the brand has become more popular and acceptable than the parent. Most people who use the product couldn't tell you who manufactures Tide detergent, and few heartburn sufferers taking Pepto Bismol or Pepcid could tell you who own those brands.

Mercedes automobiles, for example, were (pre-Chrysler merger) actually manufactured by Daimler-Benz, the names of the two founders of the company, and the name "Mercedes" was only applied in the early years after a wealthy Englishman offered to buy the entire annual production of the struggling company if the car were named after his daughter—Mercedes. The name stuck, the brand had appeal, and the company survived.

Lately, we've seen more brand association with the parent, sometimes successfully, sometimes not. In a time of increasing hostility toward drug manufacturers, Merck has taken out ads clearly linking the corporate entity with the drugs it produces to cure osteoporosis, high blood pressure, and African river blindness. Nissan, however, threatened with the popularity of its American name brand, "Datsun," changed the car's marque back to Nissan, with near-disastrous results in the marketplace. No one in America really knew what a Nissan was, or particularly wanted to drive one.

Finally, we've seen an increasing variety of products and services linked back to their ownership, in an attempt to create a brand identification (or connection) with the originator. Thus, one of the first credits you'll see on a theater screen is "An Arthur Penn film," linking the otherwise unrelated name of the movie to its director. (James Cameron was as effective as anyone could have imagined with this and related publicity techniques with "Titanic," a "brand" otherwise associated with a British steamship company, disaster, and previous films and books.) Similarly, we can find "Stan Bader's Steak House," or "Don King presents . . ." or simply "Seinfeld" (preceded by "The Donna Reed Show" and any number of eponymous programs).[1]

---

There is nothing immoral, unethical, or illegal about a consultant producing products, so long as they are high quality products and serve to help to improve the customer's condition. If they also extend the brand in that effort, what's the problem?

---

[1]One of the funniest remarks I've ever heard was muttered by Jerry Seinfeld, when he was no longer nominated for an Emmy for starring in his own show, pushed aside to make way for Michael J. Fox, then starring in "Spin City." "Apparently," observed Seinfeld, "the Academy [of Television Arts and Sciences] appears to believe that Mr. Fox was more effective and realistic playing a fictional character than I was playing myself."

How to Establish a Unique Brand in the Consulting Profession

# THE IRONCLAD CASE FOR PRODUCTS
# IN THE CONSULTING PROFESSION

There is some fastidious thinking that a consultant is above having product for sale, just like a modern doctor is above bleeding patients. However, that thinking is usually expressed by those who don't feel they can create products, and modern medicine has reverted to using leeches on wounds to assist in the clotting process.

Products can do the following in your branding strategy:

## Enhance Credibility

Many buyers will hear of a book or have one recommended to them with all of the tremendous credibility that the printed word possesses. No buyer is impressed equally by a website, which anyone can put up tomorrow. But a book implies a methodology, a thought process, many months of incubation, and a third party's (the publisher who, one presumes, is no fool) endorsement.

I was specifically invited into the Times Mirror Group and Hewlett-Packard because of my books on strategy and consulting, and those two initial projects alone were worth over a half-million dollars.

## Reach New Markets

You clearly understand who you are deliberately "reaching out to" in your marketing efforts, and you have a pretty good idea of who is likely to be attracted by your gravity efforts (or else how would you know how to structure them). However, products can be purchased by anyone, from distributors (for example, Amazon.com), your website, bookstores, alliance partners, and so on.

I was called by a pharmaceutical firm in Toronto to help them with a project. "How did you find me?" I asked, trying to find the cause of that success. "Why, my predecessor has some of your tapes in the drawer here," said the buyer, "and I listened to them. You're not bad." Apparently I wasn't good enough for his predecessor to keep the tapes, but I wasn't bad enough to have them destroyed! I got the job.

Participants in my mentoring program who establish effective newsletters consistently report business inquiries from organizations they've never heard of or didn't anticipate as potential clients. The newsletters are passed around and

I wrote a book called *Our Emperors Have No Clothes.* When it went out of print, I claimed reversion rights, and published it myself. It is listed on my website as well as on Amazon.com.

One day I received an email from the editor of a German publication in Switzerland, the largest German language business magazine in Europe.

"We need controversial pieces, which no one here can do because of cultural norms, but which you do in your book," she wrote. "Would you be willing to provide a nine-page excerpt, slightly rewritten, for $2,500?"

I was and I did. The process took about forty-five minutes. The check came one week later. The magazine followed two months later. The first inquiry from a German business came four months later.

Products build brand (in this case contrarian and controversial were the keys), and a body of work builds a body of brands.

---

shared, and their destination is often similar to that of a bottle with a message floating over the abysmal depths.

## Close Business Faster

Clients love "takeaways" and materials, often to the point of valuing a three-ring binder more than a consulting project's actual results. If you're able to provide products that can be purchased (or simply included) within the parameters of the project, you're much more able to outshine the product-less competition and close the business that much more rapidly.

During an interview with an executive vice president in a bank, I was disturbed by the fact that she was glancing distractedly through my product catalog, which was part of the press kit I had sent in advance. Finally, she said, "We'll take four hundred of these," pointing to my book on behavior and motivation. "I thought we were talking about a productivity audit," I stammered. "Oh, you're hired for that, but I wanted to make sure we could get these to our people in advance so they'd all be brought up to speed prior to the project." She hadn't even inquired about my fee.

## Create Passive Income

All consultants (especially any poor souls still charging for their time and not the value they generate for the client) dream of making money while they sleep. Products provide the passive income that enables you to invest further in your brand, expand your gravity, compensate for slow periods, plan that trip to Tahiti, or make more phone calls to your friendly broker at Charles Schwab.

Products can be sold via the Internet, through distributors, in your own catalog, on your website, during initial prospecting, at public speeches, by partners, and in a myriad of other ways. They are like an investment account, gathering interest day in and day out.

I had always thought my products were merely minor marketing aids. When I began to make five figures with them, I created a catalog. Now I'm well into six figures, with a four-color catalog, widespread distribution, and an empire of both commercial and self-publishing.

Most consultants have some combination of checklists, models, matrices, templates, workbooks, manuals, software, handouts, and other sundry performance aids, which, with a minor bit of combination, editing, and design improvement, can be turned into products.

> Products have to be effective, not complicated; valuable in improvement, not cheap in price; targeted at a market or buyer segment and not universal; and always representing you and your brand, not copycat or iterations of others' work.

## Create Reciprocal Income

Ken Blanchard was a consultant who wrote a book called *The One Minute Manager,* which led to "one-minute" nearly everything (à la today's "Chicken Soup" ubiquity). Whether it's transactional analysis, emotional intelligence, reengineering, or any other approach, the effectiveness of the product creates a plethora of additional consulting work. A famous guru, who shall go nameless, was requested by several clients for whom I also worked at an enormous fee, simply on the basis of his book. His addresses to management were often laced with epithets and worse, and he berated the management without much in the way of solid recommendations or techniques. But his schedule was full, due to the book.

Products create a tremendous "spillover" into the consulting business (and the speaking business, if you've also followed that path or use it in your gravity). More clients hire speakers on the basis of books than for any other reason short of celebrity (which is often forged by books). Speakers' bureaus will often ask an applicant immediately, "What have you written?"

## Achieve Global Appeal

More than simply "reaching new markets" as described above, products, unlike South American wines, travel very well. I've had books translated into German, Italian, and Chinese, and colleagues have topped me grandly in Japanese, Croat, Finnish, and other exotic (to me) languages. Moreover, most of the business world speaks English, and translation isn't usually even necessary.

In any one week, my website accepts orders from Botswana, Poland, Australia, and Germany. Your brand can travel at the speed of light, or at least at the speed of modern communications, and you will find yourself deriving income and creating marketing inroads in areas that are a complete surprise. I've been asked to appear in Singapore, Hong Kong, Oman, India, and dozens of other places based on product sales and awareness. There is much less risk in inviting you to consult or speak if there is an established audience familiar with your work through your products.

Without products your branding efforts will always be somewhat circumscribed. So, as the saying goes, we might as well get good at it.

# ALAN'S FAVORITE METHODS TO BOOST YOUR BRAND

## Print Products, or the Good Old Old-Fashioned Way

The computer has not done away with printed matter. It has exacerbated it. Good old hard copy, print products are very popular. If you don't believe that, just wander into your local Barnes & Noble bookstore.

We've covered publishing books commercially earlier. Let me just add here that all book contracts have a "reversion of rights" clause, meaning that if the publisher declares the book out of print (which is a fate that ultimately befalls all but a very few), the author has the right to purchase the various film and computer files and publish the book independently, removing the publisher's name and logo and replacing them with the author's. Thus, a commercially published book evolves into a self-published book after it has established an audience and repute.

You can continue to sell the work through normal distributors, with yourself as the new publisher. An added advantage is that you're moving away from the publisher's twice a year royalty payments of 15 percent or less, and toward a profit of about $23 per book at the time of sale! (You can reprint a hard cover book for about $2 to $4 per book, depending on volume, and sell them easily for $25 to $30.)

There are also specialty books. These can range from booklets you produce of fifty to seventy-five pages on topics that represent your brand: sales velocity, team building, coaching skills, diversity acceptance, etc. The advantage here is that these booklets can be produced in color for as little as a dollar or two, and can be sold for $5 to $10. Because of their inexpensive cost, they can also be given away in press kits or as gifts or marketing devices very economically.

I've had hundreds of these booklets ordered by clients and non-clients alike, spreading my name and my brand all through those organizations. My booklet *How to Maximize Fees in Professional Service Firms* is in its fourth printing, and Amazon.com orders about seventy copies a month at the moment.

Take your brand specialties—be they organizing work, humor, conflict resolution, process improvement, or whatever—and consider the creation of manuals, booklets, operating guidelines, reference works, performance aids, and other materials that can be sold to non-clients prior to a consulting sale, and to clients after a consulting sale.

---

Despite the popularity of audio, video, and electronic alternatives, the printed word and "hard copy" product is, in my experience, still the most popular purchase in the business community.

## Audiocassettes and Albums

Cassettes and cassette albums are very popular. For business use, people like cassettes that can be played on the commute in the car or on a portable player while jogging, or even in the office on the computer.

However, one of the most popular uses of cassettes, in particular, is wide distribution through similar functions, such as sales forces. Management's ability to send the same message to everyone, especially when it can be heard during "down time," is valued. I have colleagues who sell consulting projects that include monthly or quarterly cassette tapes to be provided to all people who have been involved in their projects.

A cassette product should never be a "talking head" on tape, nor should it be solely done in a studio environment. These tend to be pedantic and dry. The best cassette products have these qualities are:

- They are taped before a live audience, including audience reaction, laughter, and even questions.
- They have different voices, interviews, role plays, and similar involvement to create diversity and variety.
- They use humor, stories, and anecdotes.
- They provide solid examples and techniques, and are not merely abstract, conceptual, or "motivational." (This is important. Skills are needed to provide for improvement. Most "motivational" approaches simply attempt to rationalize failure to make the listener feel better—briefly.)

A single cassette tape may be a good marketing device, but the best products involve multiple tapes and tapes combined with print materials into "albums." Such albums have these advantages:

- They are a much better branding "platform," providing more physical space, more content, and more perceived value.
- They combine approaches to various learning styles: visual, auditory, sequential, etc.
- They can be sold for much, much higher prices. The combination of elements exponentially increases perceived value.

> Don't offer to "unbundle" sets of materials. Someone will always try to buy "only the workbook" or "just the cassettes." Simply tell them you don't do it. After all, publishers have policies and you're entitled to your own.

My highest priced products almost always combine elements: a twelve-tape, 100-page workbook combined album on marketing for $150; a 150-page book with a disk on proposals for $149; a 100-page book with CD ROM on process visuals for $75; a four-tape, two-workbook album on marketing for consultants for $120. These are just a few examples. People love to purchase "combined media," and the brand opportunity is all the greater. Expensive products are virtually never discarded, and there is the belief that one gets what one pays for.

Cassettes are inexpensive to produce (about $1 each in volume, including labels), and an album of tapes or mixed media creates a highly unique brand mechanism.

Finally, find a first-rate audio firm with sophisticated editing capabilities. With today's technology, they are readily found. If it's a mixed-media album, have your printing and even packaging competitively bid. I've found thousands of dollars of difference, because some firms themselves subcontract to expensive suppliers. Some of my booklets are printed in Minneapolis, my cassettes duplicated in Texas, and my printing done in Rhode Island. You want two things above all: control of the "look" for your brand, and control of the price for your profits.

## Video Products

This one might seem far-fetched to some of you, but we are discussing sophisticated branding techniques for highly successful consultants, so travel along for a few more minutes.

Video is a bit awkward, in that it can't be watched in the car, requires complete attention, and can become obsolete quickly (due to clothing, examples used, the environment, and so forth). It is also the province of some incredible

A man with a mellifluous Indian accent calls and asks for a review copy of one of my books. "For what publication?" I inquire.

"Oh, just for myself," he says. "If I like it, I'll purchase it."

I'm stunned for just a moment, and then I say, "This isn't a library. We sell books here. If the book isn't what it's promised to be, we'll refund your money. But we don't allow you to read our books for free."

"Why not?!" he replies, outraged. "If I like it I'll promise to pay, and if I don't, why should I keep it? Surely this is reasonable."

"There's no way that I'm doing that," I say, starting to become upset at the audacity of the request. "You'll buy it or you won't read it. And it sounds to me as if you really need it."

"That's not the way to do business!!" he shouted, and I hung up.

Several hours later, I happened to answer the phone again when that exact same accent asked, "Do you accept credit cards? I'd like to buy one of your books."

Sometimes, you just have to stick to your guns.

---

amateurism. (Recall my example about the speaker placed in front of a huge mirror reflecting the camera and crew.)

The advantage of a video, however, is that it's "three dimensional," provides the opportunity for others to extol your benefits, and creates a vibrant brand identity if done correctly (without mirrors). The product should focus on your brand expertise, and may include:

- Excerpts of you speaking in front of a group
- Brief interviews with clients who support your approaches
- Graphics and images which explain the techniques
- Actual examples (for example, a meeting being facilitated or a person being counseled)
- Mini-dramas and role plays

The key is to remember that this is a product, not a promotional video, so there must be overwhelming value in the form of clear techniques, approaches, and performance aids. Your own brand promotion should be "soft" and subtle.

Sometimes the most careful product development planning is upstaged by pure serendipity. Be sensitive to client opportunities that also can generate products on someone else's nickel.

Some of the finest video products I've seen are imperfect, in that the lighting isn't ideal, the sound is average, and the setting is not a professional studio. However, they are "live," in that a client has videotaped a presentation or speech you've done and you have a copy. With the client's permission, you can use all of this or excerpts in a video product. My videos on marketing skills and on product development (with no small irony there) were both shot in front of an audience during extensive question and answer sessions. The dynamics are wonderful and there is great energy, complete with flaws (I nearly knock a large plant right off the stage).

Brief digression for those interested in professional speaking: A demonstration video and/or audio ("demos") are essential for prospective clients and for speakers bureaus. Although many people specialize in creating these for you, the result is a "look-alike" version of what that source has generated for a hundred other speakers. My best demos were shot live by clients wanting to use them for remote sites and for new people in the future. Always include in your contracts or agreements the fact that you receive two masters of any audio and video recordings made with permission to use them for your own purposes (you may have to edit out client proprietary information). These live tapes are ideal for demos as well as products, and they are created for virtually nothing. Your only costs are for editing and packaging.[2]

---

[2]Many speakers charge extra for the right to record. I don't, but I do demand these copies. They are a good idea in any case, in the event someone later claims that you said that women are inferior or that the company should invest in Nehru jackets as a long-term strategy. It's useful to have an actual record of your comments.

For a product called "Stories I Could Never Tell," which are off-the-wall but actual experiences from my travels inappropriate for my traditional corporate audiences, I assembled thirty friends and offered them free lunch at a club I belong to. Their job was to listen to ninety minutes of my stories in front of two cameras and respond appropriately. With lunch staring them in the face in a private room, they did a marvelous job, and I was able to edit down to sixty excellent minutes. The entire production, with editing and lunch, cost about $1,500, and copies are less than $10 each of the final product.

Videos will continue to be useful products, especially with the advent of DVD and improved quality over computer screens.

## Electronic/Internet Products

I thought I was pretty clever including a disk with templates of my proposals in my proposal book (and so did the publisher) until I purchased a new Mac G3 computer and found that it didn't even accept disks. Then a reviewer told me that a new book I was preparing "cried out" for a CD-ROM and urged me to investigate. When I did, I found that the CD could be "burned" (created), edited, revised, and five hundred copies made for less than $1,400. The result is that the 100-page book sells for $75 at retail. Many people in the business are skipping videotapes entirely and recording solely on CD. (I think there is room for both.)

> People visit your website seeking value. Products should be positioned as additional value purchases, not as "goods" or "items for sale." They are simply increased value propositions for the visitor to consider.

If you are a serious consultant, you should have a website, and if you have a website, you should have products for sale. The website is one of the flagships for your brand(s), and there is no better place to reinforce the brand with product sales.

The guidelines for selling products on your website should include:

- A secure server, so that people can use credit cards with confidence
- If you have many products, use a "shopping cart" format, so that people can add products while they browse and don't have to go to an order form each time
- The color cover of each product, with a brief explanation, and an endorsement or testimonial for each, separately, with attribution
- The ability to print out the order form in case someone would prefer to fax or mail it to you
- Easy navigation among pages, so that the visitor isn't "stuck" in a certain sequence
- Acceptance of all major credit cards
- Clear instructions about whether taxes will be added, shipping charges, overseas shipping, acceptable funds, etc. (For example, I will not invoice, but only accept credit cards or checks in advance. I don't want the hassle— and expense—of invoicing, follow-up, bad debts, etc.)
- A discount offer if someone opts to buy everything (You won't get this if you don't ask, and I've found that a "take it all price" that includes a 20 percent discount generates single sales of all twenty-five or thirty products once or twice a month.)
- A return policy (you don't accept returns, you do within thirty days, satisfaction guaranteed, etc.)

A word about product sales: You will receive orders and inquiries from bookstores and buying groups, which use the ISBN number to find the publisher. You'll need to have a policy for such "wholesale" sales. Many bookstores expect deep discounts as a matter of course—and expect to be billed. My policy is that I never offer discounts on small orders, always charge for shipping, and require payment at the time of the order. The bookstores will generally pass this on to their customers, adding their own profit. But you will need to "educate" these buyers.

On your email signature file, include your latest product offering. That way, you can ensure that every time you send email, you're advertising your most recent product. All email programs have the provision for optional signature files, so you can include it only on certain correspondence and eliminate the "ad" on client correspondence, if you wish. Here's an example:

> Alan Weiss's newest book: *The Ultimate Consultant* (Jossey-Bass/Pfeiffer), now available in bookstores, at Amazon.com, or at our website: http://www.summitconsulting.com.

Here's an example of a newsletter promotion in a signature file:

> Subscribe to "Balancing Act," our free, monthly, electronic newsletter about blending life, work, and relationships by email to: join-balancingact@summitconsulting.com

Signature file "promotions," if brief and unobtrusive (do not use colors, bold headings, and so on, which are distracting and don't always translate in the recipient's software) are excellent mechanisms to sell products attached closely to your brand.

Newsletters are also viable electronic products. Although many are distributed for free (such as my "Balancing Act" above), many people sell them in conjunction with passwords or restricted access sites. Newsletters on the web tend to proliferate, since people share readily with each other, and it's virtually impossible to prevent one subscriber from providing his or her issue for free to others. However, newspapers can also be shared and that hasn't dampened their appeal. I think paid subscriber newsletters make sense as products if:

- They are packed with value and no promotion whatsoever
- They are monthly (quarterly is too infrequent, weekly is too difficult to maintain with high quality)
- They are highly targeted (for example, specifically on coaching and not on consulting in general, or specifically on commercial real estate sales and not selling in general)

Finally, there are electronic products that others produce with your intellectual property. For example, firms such as ontimetraining.com will take the books written by consultants and others and convert the content into one or more online courses, which are then sold as part of "universities" to large corporations. Every employee who accesses your course within the university generates an income stream for you.

These options are "no-brainers" as far as I'm concerned, since the online provider invests in converting your content into courses and pays you a commission. Any income derived is pure "gravy," is total profit, and the usage just may generate interest in your consulting services. The provider will even place a "portal" on your site so that visitors can access the provider's server to take your courses. (I don't recommend those online "universities" that require that you pay to have your courses converted and offered. You are already contributing your intellectual property, and you shouldn't have to invest beyond that.)

I've entered into relationships with online organizations that offer my books as courses, others that offer my videos as educational opportunities, and still others that offer my talents as an online "expert" for a given seminar.[3]

> Alliances are wonderful product boosters if 1 + 1 = 64. There must be a dramatic synergy that creates opportunity that neither partner could have seized without the other.

## Product Alliances

I'm speaking solely of product alliances here (we've already covered alliances for marketing purposes), and the difference between these and the online provider above, for example, is that with the latter you earn a commission or royalty. But in true alliances you are a partner. The key here is *synergy.*

I've had a very successful alliance with Kennedy Information, which is one of the leading publishers of newsletters, industry reports, and analyses for consulting, recruiting, human resources, IT, and related fields. For several

---

[3]When I've done online presentations interactively, I can see a screen that alternates among the several dozen sites participating. It's somewhat unsettling to see an occasionally empty room or a person asleep, but you get used to it!

years I published in newsletters such as *Consultant's News*. One day, the CEO, Wayne Cooper, and I decided to see if there were collaborations possible. Kennedy had vast marketing and "reach"; I had several prominent brands ("Million Dollar Consulting," "the contrarian," etc.) and a significant brand loyalty.

We decided on three major collaborations within our alliance: publishing very high-end books to form a library on specific subjects[4]; producing a new, practice management newsletter[5]; and a series of seminars on selling consulting services, called The Rainmaker™ series. So, three products emerged: books, a newsletter, and seminars. We split the profits on the books according to a formula, I'm paid to edit the newsletter, and we split the profits from the seminars after all expenses.

I never could have reached the Kennedy audience on my own. They could not have provided the expertise for the products from within. The synergy was perfect. Our books sell at a premium ($149) and we have a hard time keeping them on the shelves. The newsletter generates interest in both of our operations and in additional products. And the seminars, lucrative in and of themselves, generate high levels of interest in in-house seminars, consulting help, my mentoring program, product sales, etc.

Once you've established a valuable and recognizable brand, you can seek out such alliance partners, who can extend your reach and provide further product options, in addition to promoting current products. I think that the criteria for a sound alliance must include the following:

*Total Trust.* You have to be able to trust your partner with your wallet. As extensive as contracts and written agreements may be, they can all be abrogated and broken. You must trust your partner implicitly and the chemistry must be totally comfortable. Whenever there is the least question of ethics (for example, a seminar client requests a one-off variation), Kennedy and I discuss it openly and arrive at a win/win/win outcome.

---

[4]These have since been published as *How to Write a Proposal That's Accepted Every Time; How to Market, Establish a Brand, and Sell Services*; and *How to Acquire New Business and Expand Existing Business.*

[5]*What's Working in Consulting,* a monthly.

One brand I've scrupulously developed is "high priced." I believe people think they get what they pay for, and I want to be seen as the Mercedes of the business.

At a book fair, the person in charge of my sales asked if the $149 price on my proposal book was a misprint. Was it really $14.90?

"No," I replied loudly, within earshot of some potential buyers, "that book is the best value in the entire building. Imagine spending only $149 to gain $40,000 or more on your proposals?!"

A little later I overheard one visitor comment to another, "Come with me. I want to show you the best value in the place," as she headed for my table.

I've been told that only someone with my courage—or chutzpah—would charge $149 for a 100-page softcover book. I think anyone who believes in himself or herself and who truly understands the power of branding will do so in a minute.

If you don't believe your brand, who will?

*Top-Level Relationship.* The relationship must be with the top person in the alliance partner. You may work with many others and see them more often, but the relationship must be with the ultimate "buyer." You are the principal in your firm, and you must be a peer of the principal in the partnering firm.

*Clear Financial Understandings.* Don't leave anything to chance here. Create clear rules for revenue splits, expense underwriting, promotion charges, and so forth. This doesn't have to be a legal document, but it does have to be in writing. Don't wait for the awkward situation where a client says, "I'm willing to spend $150,000 for a customized version," and you then realize that one partner will be investing more than the other in this outcome will. Think of all contingencies beforehand.

*Periodic Review.* Agree to discuss the arrangements once a quarter, preferably in person. You'll both have other priorities on your own radar screens, so it's essential to make time even when the relationship and the alliance seem to be going swimmingly (you don't want to meet only when there are problems). One of the main reasons for these reviews is to determine how to raise the bar, and create still more synergy: customized products, additional workshops, higher technology, new markets, etc.

---

> Treat your alliance partner as you would your best clients. Take nothing for granted, build the relationship constantly, and continue to offer value. Also, don't be afraid to "push back" when you must.

*Create an "Out" Option.* Nothing lasts forever, especially if your own goals change, your alliance partner is sold, or some other unexpected force intervenes. There's nothing dishonorable about an escape clause for either side. Determine in advance what each partner must do to intelligently and professionally end the relationship—there may be financial remuneration, non-compete, timing, and other considerations. It's best to determine this at the outset.

Alliances are best entered into when you don't need them. Think about it. You must have the wherewithal to walk away or reject certain terms. You can't do that as easily early in your career, when you might view an alliance as an urgent need to propel you to the next level. But at this point in your career, you are in a position to rely on the power of your brands and the repute that you bring to the table.

One final admonition: Keep your basic consulting practice out of the alliance arrangements. Use the alliance for brand exposure, product distribution, and penetration of new markets. Don't, however, compromise the basis of your current achievements by combining it with another firm. That will serve to mute or confuse your brand, not to promote it. My consulting work can only be obtained by dealing directly with my company. No alliance partner, broker, course provider, or web presence has the authority or the power to represent me in that capacity.

## BRAND NEW LESSONS

Product sales are not in bad taste and are never inappropriate for a consultant, although you may surely choose not to indulge in this device. However, I urge you to consider it.

Products are "automatic" brand enhancers. The brand(s) you've established promote the product, and the product, in turn, reinforces the brand. My advice is to pursue a sequence something like this:

1. Establish print products, preferably a book and/or booklets
2. Use your website to promote these products
3. Seek other distribution methods for the printed products (for example, Amazon.com, others' websites, online publishers, online training firms, etc.)
4. As opportunity arises, create audio and/or video products
5. Create combined albums of print, audio, and/or video
6. Consider electronic products and newsletters
7. When you have a "critical mass" of products or potential offerings, seek an alliance partner who can add marketing, distribution, and promotion to your own efforts

There comes a time when you might want to slow down or "retire" (whatever that means in this business). Products are the constituents of a fine passive income for those periods. Or their revenues can be used merely to finance vacations or investment opportunities, or the kids' college funds. If you're considering the sale of the business some day, product revenues do constitute an ongoing cash flow and valuable asset, if their ownership in included in the sale.

Products simply provide you with more flexibility—and more of an opportunity to expand your brand. If you can do that, and make money besides, it certainly seems like a wise course.

A new client once told me, "When I saw you had written a book on behavior, I just had to meet you. To me, writing a book is so difficult, so unthinkable, that I just can't imagine how one goes about it." The client was the CEO of a company that worked with NASA, and he couldn't understand how I could write a book.

# CHAPTER 9

# Where Are We Heading and How Do We Capitalize?

## *A Dozen Trends That Close the Case for Branding*

I've tried to establish in prior chapters that branding isn't a fad or short-lived trend. However, while branding has been a long-term product device, it hasn't been as widely used in services, and it is still in its infancy in terms of consulting services. That is the main benefit for consultants today, particularly entrepreneurs, small firm owners, and successful solo practitioners.

Branding is like any other consulting tactic, in that it must be aimed at the future, not the past. No one is vitally interested today in reengineering, or "right brain/left brain" thinking, or emotional intelligence. These are among the myriad of fads that peak and ebb in the sea of change. Clients and potential buyers will continue to be focused on the basics of their business: heightened productivity, greater profitability, increased market share, better retention of talent, deeper customer loyalty, competing in the global market, appealing to increasingly diverse customer bases, and so forth.

I believe that there are some clear developing patterns among our clients and within our profession that will be the fuel for future branding efforts. Some are threats, perhaps, but like all threats, also represent opportunity to those who are willing to take prudent risk and exploit change. Most will be applicable to any kind of practice and a wide variety of consulting expertise and skills. My advice is to give each one careful consideration before prematurely determining "that doesn't apply to me."

Most consultants didn't think the Internet applied to them whenever it was that Al Gore stated he first invented it!

## THE TRENDS

### Trend #1: Increasing Stimuli

Depending on what source you choose to consider, the average buyer of consulting services is probably exposed to between three thousand and five thousand commercial messages or advertisements each day. Most of these are not specifically consulting messages, of course, but nonetheless they are all inputs to the sensory system in one form or another screaming for the buyer's attention. Branding is increasingly required to stand out in this crowd—or cacophony—of publicity.

Globally, this number is also growing, thanks to the Internet, the proliferation of global business, multi-nationals, and the "Americanization" of the business scene. Any type of capitalistic system or commercial economy will generate more and more "noise" for potential buyers.

It is estimated that one weekday edition of the *New York Times* contains more information than an inhabitant of the 16th Century processed *in an entire lifetime.* The 16th Century was not chopped liver: It was the time of the Renaissance, Erasmus, exploration, and Martin Luther. However, information overload, despite all the "newness," was not a problem. It's an increasing problem today.

> We are surrounded by so much attention-demanding "noise" as consumers that we're both weary of people calling our name and bored with attempts to secure our attention. The customer's focus is not as easy to obtain as it used to be.

What is a consultant today? Is it really the mega-merger, former accounting and audit firms, which still bear a strong financial mentality and rarely could be accused of performing real organization development consulting? Is it the consulting arms of once-pure high-tech consumer product providers, such as IBM and HP? What about the moonlighting college professor, or the academic who's written a totally impractical book that is nevertheless seized on by people who haven't read it as the latest anodyne and panacea? Do consultants need credentials, like architects or landscapers, or can anyone simply hang out that shingle?

This confusion is going to increase, not decrease, in the years ahead. I deal with people in my mentoring program around the world, every day, who express difficulty in "establishing their credibility" and "gaining respectability." (And their response, all too often, is to lower fees and/or take the position of a vendor, which further weakens their position in no small irony.) As a successful consultant, you've gained credibility and respectability, one would hope, but it needs to be solidified and perpetuated through your branding efforts.

Speed and accuracy of message to the potential buyer's mind is of the essence. Many years ago it might have required—justifiably—many months to establish the right level of intimacy and to deliver the correct message for any given buyer. Today, the exigencies of business and the rapidity of communications have reduced that time to days. It was not unusual for me, even ten years ago, to spend six months building a trusting relationship. Today, I'm sometimes able to do it in one meeting. The buyer needs speed, because market pressures are pressing. And I'm able to collapse the relationship time because my brand precedes me.

*Note: "I've heard of you" always beats "who are you?"*

## Trend #2: Proliferation of Products, Services, and Their Brands

I always hesitate to say, "Do it because everyone else is," but there's a certain merit to that argument for branding. Take a look at store shelves, magazine advertisements, buyer's guide listings, billboards, Internet banners, or whatever other metric you care to use. You'll find that brands are growing at an enormous pace, because it has been established that branding is an effective way to reach potential buyers. This will continue in present and future communications media.

Ballparks no longer simply have billboards with advertisers. Those stadium sites now have rotating arrangements, so that several brands and advertisers can be shown each few minutes. Streaming banners and "click through" devices appear on a growing number of websites as companies such as Burst Multimedia and Doubleclick provide specialty content web advertising.

Not long ago my wife told me to go buy my own breakfast cereal, since I had made the critical error of criticizing her choices. "How difficult could this be?" I smugly thought, and drove off for what I assumed would be a fifteen-minute excursion. An hour later, I returned from long aisles packed with more conceivable combinations of oats, wheat, corn, rice, fruit, nuts, roughage, vitamins, government-approved artificial ingredients, and who knows what else than I could ever have imagined. When I unpacked my three boxes, two of them were what my wife had already purchased, and the third wasn't really cereal but some kind of wheat germ topping.

---

The amazing thing isn't so much the proliferation of brands, but the fact that so many brands can co-exist with an integrity and singularity about their attributes.

---

"Designer" breweries have certainly demonstrated the potential to release innumerable brands that retain their own uniqueness and, one hopes, following and loyalty.

The reaction to "What kind of consultant are you" is too often a detailed response of methodology and approaches that bores the potential buyer to tears and can't possibly be expressed in print very economically or dynamically. It's far better to allow your brand to do the talking. (Which is also why the ultimate brand is your name, since it's immediately singular and non-copyable.)

*Note: If someone says, "Oh, yeah, I know quite a few consultants just like you," your brand is too weak.*

## Trend #3: Continuing Lack of Certification

There is absolutely nothing on the horizon that indicates that consultants will be regulated, certified, licensed, approved, or otherwise housebroken according to any governmental or professional body. In fact, all the signs are for the reverse: continued anarchy. This is because:

- No one will agree on criteria, because consulting is so fractious (from expert witnesses to continuous flow experts to strategy retreat facilitators)

# VIGNETTE

Trade associations and professional groups are like the boy scouts and girl scouts of our youth—they place an emphasis on merit badges and the colorful patches that we can wear on our "uniform."

The National Speakers Association, for example, has the designation CSP (Certified Speaking Professional) and CPAE Hall of Fame Member (Colleagues' Peer Award of Excellence). Accompany that with one's "legitimate" credentials (Ph.D. or M.D.) and you have an introduction something like this: "Please welcome to the stage CSP, CPAE Hall of Fame Member, Ph.D., Joan Lamont."

After about a dozen of these, not only is the audience yawning, but the agenda is slipping behind!

Now, ask any client if he or she has heard of the speaking or consulting designation (Certified Management Consultant, Certified Professional Consultant to Management, and so on) and not only will he or she likely say "no," but also definitely say that he or she doesn't care!

We love our merit badges, but forget that branding is in the eye of the beholder/buyer.

- There is not a high level of trust (Will those influencing certification criteria also be skewing them toward their own advantage or to the most powerful lobby's advantage?)
- Historic attempts have been disasters (ACME, IMC, etc.) and have formed a precedent that the profession is incapable of organizing itself
- Most pointedly, the buyer doesn't seem to care; there is absolutely no call from the client to regulate or unify the consulting profession
- Unlike, say, law, finance, or medicine, there is no canonical basis for even rudimentary criteria of effectiveness. A heart operation, balance sheet, or motion for discovery all have to follow certain precedent and procedure. Not so for a focus group, executive coaching, or competitive analysis. The beauty—and the results—are in the eye of the beholder.

Consultants don't want to regulate themselves, the government isn't really interested beyond certain tax-imposing potential, and, most critically, the buyers don't care. There is absolutely no impetus for consultants to be subject to licensing.

Given these realities, branding is the road out of the swamp. Differentiation in this profession is difficult, and there are no umbrella bodies that guarantee competency (for example, a physician or surgeon can also pass graduate "boards") or that provide for self-policing and ethics conformity (for example, the American Bar Association). Therefore, the greatest differentiator and most assured guarantee of excellence is a brand that is recognized and sought out.

*Note: When people know of you and your brand through word of mouth—when there is a recognition factor—you also gain instant credibility in their eyes.*

## Trend #4: Cost-Effectiveness and Economies of Scale

The problem with a global economy and a proliferation of buyers is that it can be much harder to reach them. If your buyer were the vice president of sales in an insurance company, then you knew how to ask for him or her at the switchboard, to whom to write, what trade associations the buyer belonged to, what publications the buyer likely read, and so on. This was a discrete, highly identifiable target.

Today, however, the combination of downsizing, title changes, cross-functional collaboration, globalization, and changing market needs has created chaos. Someone whose expertise lies in sales skills, for example, might find that the highest potential buyers are managers of call response centers; team leaders in telemarketing operations; vice presidents of geographic areas; or even CEOs of start-up dotcom companies.

We are all process consultants in many respects, with abilities and expertise that cut across functions, hierarchies, and industries. Consequently, the chaos also affords advantages in terms of a myriad of new and growing buying points. But how does one target a rather amorphous cloud, instead of that highly visible vice president of insurance sales?

---

> The growing ambiguity of the marketplace and of buyers is a wonderful beneficence to consultants *if* they know how to lure buyers to them, rather than try to find the buyers in the fog.

The "gravity" approach I provided earlier is an attempt to provide a beacon and fog horn in the overcast. The key to this new proliferation of potential buyers is to lure them to you, and not get lost yourself in the fog trying to find them as though you were Diogenes looking for an honest man.

Your brand is your beacon. It becomes the most cost-effective, widespread, and greatest gravity device that you possess. You should be using it to attract the most qualified buyers out of the increasing numbers of prospects in the evolving economy.

*Note: You can catch fish by diving after them and chasing one with a spear, but casting a net filled with bait will enable you to select the biggest and most satisfying with minimal effort.*

## Trend #5: Business-to-Business Acumen and Recognition Is Exploding

The Internet has created a heightened sensitivity to "business-to-business" marketing. This has been erratically satisfied on the web, which seems like an ideal, fast, accessible medium for business-to-business transactions, but lacks the relationship building that is often required in a service context.

It's one thing to buy staples or even computers on a price and convenience basis, but it's quite another to secure the services of an attorney, accountant, or consultant. I don't care who sees my electrical outlets, but I care a lot about who sees my books.

When businesses seek safety in acquiring services, branding is a paramount consideration for the buyer and a potent weapon for the seller. "Get me IBM" (or, perhaps today, Microsoft) was a purchasing manager's mantra, just as "Let's get McKinsey" might be a CEO's visceral response to a strategy challenge. When a buyer (or a buyer's boss, even more powerfully) says, "We'll need some sales training" (or competitive intelligence, or executive coaching, or operations audit), that launches a general search that may or may not embrace your offerings. But when that buyer says, "Get me Alan Weiss" (or "the contrarian," or "the team builder," or "The Telephone Doctor™"[1]), that search has already been awarded to that brand.

> Business-to-business transactions are, perhaps, even more sensitive to brand power and implications than the typical consumer, since the buying business has probably tried to foster its own brand for similar purposes.

Brand development has become a strategic issue for business-to-business providers, but it's even more of an essential element for service providers, where relationship building will remain a key component of the buying decision. An effective brand and repute can shortcut this process with a demand for the particular brand rather than the generalized service.

*Note: People still say, "Do you have a Kleenex?" and not "Do you have a Kleenex brand tissue?" or "Do you have a facial tissue?" Thus, "Can we get Alan Weiss?" is far better than being considered only after the question: "Can we get a strategy consultant?"*

---

[1]Nancy Friedman, a real person and a real brand, alluded to earlier.

## Trend #6: The Great Advantage in, and Fascination with, Being Numero Uno

Every time Avis's very intelligent marketing campaign stated, "We're number two, so we have to try harder," they were inescapably giving promotion to the number one, which everyone knew to be Hertz. Organizations have long wasted effort and resources trying to "catch" a number one competitor who, sometimes for reasons beyond rationality (longevity, consumer fickleness, accident of geography), was uncatchable.

My advice to clients who do not lead their segment is always the same: Create a new segment or niche is which you are number one by dint of your singular achievement in that tailored niche. Those resources are far better spent than in any attempt to overtake a competitor with an insurmountable lead.

In consulting, it's only (and only theoretically) possible to be "number one" if you're an Andersen competing on size, or a McKinsey relying on repute, or an IBM utilizing brute strength and a brilliant brand. For 99.9 percent of us, it's important to create a "numero uno" mentality among our buyers without subjecting ourselves to races we can't win and tests of strength we can't endure.

---

Most buyers will want to think they're dealing with the best. That's why an effective pricing strategy is to position yourself in the upper echelon. That works, as long as you produce at that level. For branding, the same applies: Position yourself at the top, then look and act the part. As far as I'm concerned, there is no viable alternative for successful consultants.

---

The buyer will pay more for the best, and it's up to you, via your brand, to demonstrate that you are the best. You don't have to be the biggest, the fastest, the tallest, or the richest. You only have to be *the absolute best alternative at that time for that buyer's specific needs.* An effective, recognized brand will do this for you.

The proliferation of consultants and the need for consultants has also created a fear that the people providing the services might not be first-rate. I've estimated, in fact, that upwards of 50 percent of all consultants actually aren't very good, don't have a consistent consulting model, and don't have the competencies that the client already possesses. However, *I also estimate that at least 90 percent of the buyers don't confidently know how to tell the difference*, which explains the presence of so many poor consultants and the phenomena of so many bungled projects.

We can strike the fear from the buyer's heart and raise our own immediate profile with powerful branding. I can't tell you how many times a prospect has said, "Of course, I've heard of Summit Consulting Group" or "I'm familiar with your work." They might have and might be, or they might have been told by a trusted subordinate just the day before, but that's fine with me. It means that I'm already number one for their purposes, at that moment—and that's all that counts.

Branding will assist you in being "situationally number one" at the point of sale, and that's the key.

*Note: Branding should establish you as the best in whatever niche you select for whatever buyers you select. Hence, multiple brands are effective devices to create differing "numero unos."*

## Trend #7: The Value Equation

As the economy improves—and despite dips and reversals, it's overall trend will be upward for quite some time as global markets open and technology eases access—more money will be available for services that were "luxuries" or even considered irrelevant before. Even today, we see rapid expansion of consulting and consultants into such areas as:

- Very small businesses (under $5 million)
- Third- and fourth-world countries (infrastructure and education)
- Legal complexities (expert witnesses)
- Non-traditional organizations (telecommuters and outsourcing)
- Mentoring and coaching (entrepreneurs and executives)

Something is only a luxury until it's been successfully applied—once. After that, it becomes a necessity. Hence, automatic garage openers, 100-channel cable access, expensive writing implements, personal digital assistants, cell phones, and a myriad of other products and services have become "essential" no matter what their cost.[2]

---

Strong earning power creates the opportunity to seek out heretofore unattainable value. Such value is almost always associated with luxury branding.

---

Increased amounts of discretionary income at both corporate and individual levels enable buyers to seek what would have been unattainable value under less robust circumstances. That value will be far above the pragmatic or even desired levels, and will be focused on emotional gratification at the emotional level. Hence, brand names on the consumer side—Rolex, Bulgari, Armani, Brioni, Ferrari, Aston Martin—will possess even greater cachet.

On the business side, a McKinsey may become a viable choice, whereas the firm was once thought too expensive for a particular buyer or client. Your branding, and the excellence and heights that it applies, will similarly attract more and more qualified buyers as those buyers' conditions improve.

In fact, your brands will serve as a beacon of quality during poorer times for the smaller market segment that is still buying, and as a primary attraction during better times when more and more buyers want what they couldn't have before. A brand is like a buoy, which will rise and fall with the tide but will always be visible on the surface.

Over the past several years, the American "middle class" has been represented in surveys as concerned that the economic boom has passed it by, because while essentials are easily affordable, a "better life style" is sometimes just beyond their reach. When asked about the components of a better life style—not luxury or affluence, but just a better life style—the responses included: an SUV as a second or third vehicle; large-screen, high definition television;

---

[2]One of the bizarre problems of a vibrant economy is that even exotic items, from Ferraris to Bulgari watches, are in short supply because of increased perceived value and accessibility.

additional cell phones; private schools at primary and secondary level; a third vacation.

A luxury is a luxury until the neighbors have it.

*Note: Value will always help you to stand out in a crowd, whether the crowd is well-dressed or not. Quality is always a sought-after attribute.*

## Trend #8: Focus on Output, Not Input

We've mentioned earlier Kodak's breakthrough focus on "memories" and not film, and the shampoo industry focusing on repeat usage for best results, thereby doubling consumption. In the years ahead, a growingly sophisticated and educated buyer will be most interested in the result after the purchase. The move is already underway to defocus on "deliverables," days, and time and materials, and to focus instead on results, changes, improvements, innovation, and an overall better future state.

Branding should migrate toward those results. When Gordon Bethune took over as CEO of Continental Airlines, the company was probably the absolute last choice for business travelers. Service was awful, reflecting dismal morale and a confusion about objectives (for example, first class luxury carrier or cut rate, no frills bus in the sky). Bethune clarified the airline's role—which I would characterize as effective transportation for primarily business travelers—and arrived at indices that would create that brand for the traveling public: on-time service, accurately delivered baggage, minimum customer complaints, and so forth. He determined that the company had to be number 1 or number 2 in every category, and then rewarded every employee when the goal was made. Today, Continental is the top choice of the business flyer.

---

The more a brand is associated with a certain result, the more powerful the gravity. Increasingly, buyers will be looking for results and not simply tasks.

---

Bethune looked at the required results and built his brand around it. (United's "friendly skies" doesn't work if the experience isn't actually friendly, and it too often hasn't been.) Your own brands should focus on the results you deliver, no matter how gently. "Effective Teams" is better than "Team Training," and "Teams That Create Customers" is better than either. A brand's test in consulting will increasingly be: What will you have done for me after you've gone?

*Note: You must "walk the brand's talk." You can't be "the morale builder" and fail to resolve client conflicts. Build a brand that you exemplify in every single client engagement.*

## Trend #9: Differentiation Will Be Still More Valuable Than Categorization

Consultants have seemed to take a perverse pleasure in emphasizing that they are "OD consultants," or "executive coaches," or "strategists," or specialists in "performance improvement." I've had some consulting clients who have invested a great deal in proclaiming their expertise in pharmaceuticals, or high tech, or small business markets.

# VIGNETTE

On a US Airways flight to Washington, DC, the pilot announced that a light was indicating that our landing gear would not deploy and lock. Although probably a light malfunction, he told us that we would dump all excess fuel and that the flight attendants would instruct us in the brace position. We would also divert to Dulles Airport, which had longer runways and better emergency capability.

The plane was desperately silent. Then the pilot added, "And by the way, as luck would have it, I practiced just last week in the flight simulator landing this aircraft with wheels up. So I'm confident that we'll be fine."

"What a relief," the lady next to me exhaled, "what are the odds of that?"

Very, very long, but I didn't want to mention that to her and disturb her newfound peace of mind. The pilot "brand" is so strong that lying or even fudging the truth would be unthinkable.

The problem, of course, is that such branding creates category awareness, *but not specific firm awareness*, category branding, *but not individual branding*. As consulting and consultants proliferate, even once-narrow fields are occupied by more and more competitors. I'm seeing increased competition in what were once rather arcane practices such as EEOC audits, customer response center improvement, and contract compliance reviews, to name a few.

The brand can't simply define a category; it must define an alternative. Pepsi doesn't want to proclaim that it's another cola drink; it wants to be a clear alternative to Coke (which was the ongoing problem of another, little known competitor, RC). Greyhound buses spent a fortune on electronic reservations and scheduling to improve the ease of buying a bus ticket and making bus travel easier, when all the public really wanted was a reliable, easy-to-find, long distance bus—in essence, the old Greyhound.

---

The brand is—or should be—you. That's why an individual name is the perfect differentiator. If you can't use your name, then find something else that is uniquely about you and your results.

---

Boston Consulting Group didn't simply promote its strategy business, it developed its unique and now-famous strategy quadrant, which got everyone talking about "dogs" and "cash cows." Some firms choose shareholder value as their differentiator, others choose global strategy. What can you create in a brand that doesn't attract people to your category or even your skill sets, but to you and your firm in particular?

*Note: Burger King builds its restaurants across the street from McDonald's. If you build even a successful generic or category brand, others will rush in to dilute your market. But there is only one FedEx that absolutely gets things there overnight. (No one says to a subordinate, "Airborne this package" or "Let's DHL this."*

## Trend #10: Attention Spans Will Be Briefer and Buyers More Fickle

We associate a "brand" with a mark burned into the hide of an animal to make it identifiable and recognizable to others who might encounter the animal when the owner is not also present. Our own brands should be "burned into" the potential buyer's mentality, because we're almost never likely to be present when certain needs arise for which we are the ideal solution.

Ironically, the distance from the seller (the consultant) to the purchaser (the corporate economic buyer) is farther than ever before, while that same buyer's attention span is briefer than ever before. Few consultants can still afford the luxury of marketing only in their own back yards, and many consultants now market on a global basis. Buyers, in turn, are besieged not only with the increasing barrage of messages noted above, but are also "fractured" among business demands, life balance realities, continually increasing their abilities and education, new competition, unpredictable business climates, and so on.

The remote buyer's ability—even if willing—to focus on your message is severely constrained. Therefore, it's vital that your brand be:

- Simple
- Frequently heard and seen in varied media
- Associated with the buyer's immediate needs
- Highly tactical, no matter how strategic it also may be

Loyalty, ironically, will work best with fractured, harried, and fickle buyers. It will be most comfortable to engage a "sure thing" than to try a new and risky alternative. The key is to remind the buyer of his or her own loyalty!

A simple message that is seen regularly and connected to immediate benefit will tend to be much more effective than irregular, conceptual, strategic, "big hits." Invest your resources in frequent contact, no matter how modest, not in one-time extravaganzas.

*Note: The test of highly effective branding in a market of remote buyers is that the buyer contacts you even when unsure that you are the right alternative, trusting the consultant to help determine whether a project is appropriate. That is brand loyalty par excellence.*

# Trend #11: Bang-Bang Responsiveness

Brands will be best promoted, supported, and exploited through rapid response: response to inquiries, problems, questions, vague contacts, crises, and everything in between.

Responsiveness is *the* Achilles' heel of most consulting operations. In an age of cell phones, fax machines, computers, personal digital assistants, and every other imaginable personal communications option, consultants don't communicate well. I'm astonished every week by the number of prospects and clients who thank me profusely for simply calling them back.

I return all of my calls within ninety minutes, and all of my emails within the same day (these standards pertain to my local business hours only, of course), and I hit those metrics 99 percent of the time. In fact, I usually return calls within the hour and emails within the half-day. This responsiveness once supported my brands but has now become a brand in itself. One referral endorsement to a new client said, "He is the most responsive consultant I've ever worked with."

Naturally, prospects interpret that early responsiveness as the quality of support they'll receive after they've become clients, and they're right to do so.

> Your brand can't simply sit there, like a potted plant or a doorstop. It must be organic, dynamic, and interactive. Rapid responsiveness brings your brand to life for the client.

Bring your brand to life by providing vivid examples of its actual application. If your brand is about communications, you had better be responsive and accurate; if it's about competitive intelligence, you had better have done a great deal of homework about your prospect; if it's about team building, you must interact well in your initial meeting with a prospect's committee.

*Note: Your brand isn't a statement, it's you. I recently called a sales consulting firm that didn't get back to me and had a poor receptionist. Ask yourself, "How would a prospect know my brand if I didn't actually name it?"*

## Trend #12: Brands Must Be Continually Enhanced to More Elite Status

Before you complain that you don't want an elite status because you want to focus on the middle market or some such thing, please read on. I'm talking here about the perception of increased value and status, not necessarily increased investment or more difficult access.

Cross pens were usurped by Mont Blanc as the status writing implement; Cadillac was eclipsed by Mercedes; Pan Am went out of business, despite originating international passenger service; Avon has had to change its sales and distribution method because most women now work outside the home instead of waiting, like Donna Reed, to have coffee with their neighbor who's selling cosmetics.

A brand name isn't in and of itself sufficient, and changing times threaten every brand with the ramifications of new technology, shifting buyer preferences, changed perceptions, new fashions, and more experiences. As your brand achieves success, you should work to improve its image and increase the perception of high quality, no matter what your market, because high quality best survives changing times. In our examples above, only Avon has had continuing high quality, which has enabled it to change its market and brand application. Cross, Pan Am, and Cadillac all suffered terrible quality problems, and Cross and Cadillac are still paying for them (Pan Am having been put out of its misery).

> There is nothing wrong with elitism and there is everything wrong with too-easy acquisition. You should be qualifying your buyers for the applicability of your brand to the same extent that they are qualifying you.

Mercedes successfully went "down market" with less expensive vehicles without damaging its marque one iota. Ferrari licenses its logo for inexpensive clothing and accessories. You will still be able to acquire projects at any fee level you desire, but the key is to be able to choose fee levels consciously, and not have to enter into price competition.

The time to grow your brand's image still more is when it's most successful. Don't demean it by compromise or by accepting all the business you can, no matter what its quality. Salvatore Dali, the artist, seriously undermined the long-term value of his work by turning out a bewildering assortment of creations, seemingly putting his name to almost anything. In the long term, that strategy diminished his art, his value, and his repute.

Don't allow your brand's success to plateau. The future will be about excellence and value. Keep boosting your image.

*Note: Some people are calling me "the rock star of consulting." That began to bother me, considering that I'm over 50. Then I realized that Mick Jagger is older than I am, and decided not to worry about it. Life is short. While you're here, keep your brand moving upward.*

## BRAND NEW LESSONS

Here are the key future trends affecting consulting brands and their perception:

**Trend #1:** Increasing stimuli
**Trend #2:** Proliferation of products, services, and their brands
**Trend #3:** Continuing lack of certification
**Trend #4:** Cost-effectiveness and economies of scale
**Trend #5:** Business-to-business acumen and recognition is exploding
**Trend #6:** The great advantage in, and fascination with, being numero uno
**Trend #7:** The value equation
**Trend #8:** Focus on output, not input
**Trend #9:** Differentiation will be still more valuable than categorization
**Trend #10:** Attention spans will be briefer and buyers more fickle
**Trend #11:** Bang-bang responsiveness
**Trend #12:** Brands must be continually enhanced to more elite status

How many of these are you preparing for, are you currently well positioned for, or are you even now thinking about? What can you do tomorrow to take advantage of the future?

# CHAPTER 10

# Leapfrogging

## How to Take Your Brands and Your Plans to New Heights

So, what's in the future for you? We've already established that branding isn't a fad, but it is a relatively new phenomenon for the consulting profession. And we've discussed some likely trends. The point of view to leave this book with is not "What can I do about it?" but rather "How can I lead?"

There is a profound difference between "fixing" your position and "raising the bar" to new heights. The relative positions are shown in Figure 10.1.

In the first graph, we bring our practice to a state "where it should have been." In the second graph, we raise our practice to ever-higher levels. The second involves somewhat more risk than the first: What if we don't reach that level? What if we've misjudged our brand and/or the prospects' receptivity?

However, this book (and this entire series) is for successful, sophisticated practitioners seeking to steadily improve. Therefore, the risk is probably prudent and the degree of potential reward significant. If you don't raise your own bar, no one else is going to do it for you.

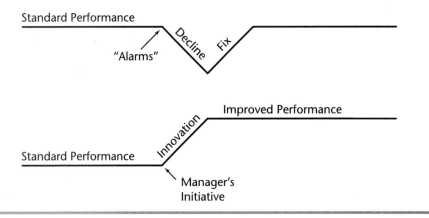

**Figure 10.1.** Fixing vs. Innovating

If you don't toot your own horn, there is no music.

In the remainder of the book, we'll discuss some techniques, approaches, ideas, and creativity to "leap frog" the branding process.

## MULTIPLE BRANDS

Too many consultants put all of their emphasis on a single brand. Even if your name is your brand—as stated earlier, one of the most desirable states—there is no contradiction in establishing additional brands. The Procter & Gamble philosophy of ensuring that their multiple brands compete against each other for customer attention, rather than with competing brands, is also appropriate and feasible for consultants.

There are two basic positions for multiple brands: independent and linked.

### Independent Brands

In this strategy, your brands are independently aimed at different markets and/or buyers, for which and for whom a synergy among the brands isn't

How to Establish a Unique Brand in the Consulting Profession

important or even of value. Here are four examples of where and when this makes sense:

1. You wish to keep your brands separate because one could damage the other. For example, a strong brand in training might preclude you from ever dealing with strategy or executive consulting. Being well-known as a coach might imperil organization development work. Separate brands with distinctive support systems (for example, different websites, different articles and placement, different speaking audiences, and so forth) serve to help create parallel avenues.

2. You are building an organization and wish to segment the attributes and assets by market. Your personal brand would demand a higher premium and focus on specialized assignments. The staff might support and implement a completely different brand or set of brands. In this way, you don't run the risk of your own powerful brand being attenuated through subordinates' direct involvement with it.

3. You may wish to separate your product offerings from your service offerings. Your books, tapes, and other passive income vehicles may be promoted with one brand (I wouldn't advise it, but think of the power of the "Idiot" brand for books ranging from computers to strategy), and your consulting services with another. In this way, you can attack both the mass market and the high-end individualized buyer with distinct vehicles.

4. You seek to remove the onus of what your strongest suit is. This sounds counter-intuitive, but if you've happened to build a very strong brand in, say, team building, and you find you can also serve well as an expert witness, there would be considerable confusion attempting to incorporate this diversity within one brand. Moreover, the power of the longer-lived and original brand will tend to overwhelm the newer brand, so separation makes eminent sense.

## Linked Brands

This approach provides for brands that may have differing markets but are enhanced by the synergy of belonging to a greater whole, or by being under a common "umbrella." Here are some examples:

1. Your name is the common attraction, and you use that for strategic advantage while creating differing brands for tactical gains. Hence, you might create "John Jones' Team Power," "John Jones' Selling Power," and "John Jones' Service Power" as individual workshops or consulting interventions tied together by the common name.

2. You are seeking leverage from a common root. For example, this book you're now reading is part of the "Ultimate Consultant" series on consulting. Each book has a different name, but there are common elements about the look and layout and an inclusion under the overall series name. If a buyer becomes enamored with one brand in a series, there is a higher probability of crossover to other brands within the same series.

3. You are making additions or acquisitions to your basic business and, while retaining the unique selling points of each, you also desire to integrate them into a common organization. Training organizations have traditionally merged other technologies into the corporate brand while continuing the individual brands in the market.

4. You are seeking to go "upscale" or "downscale," based on the quality of your original brand offerings. Mercedes moved down into lower and lower price strata while building on the original marque's high quality. Johnny Walker moved upscale from "red" to "black" to "gold" and finally "blue" in the liquor market, always within the overall brand image. In this way, you can leverage earlier client work into new fields of work by associating the brands either closely or at a distance.

> You can have an indefinite number of brands, some linked and others quite independent. In fact, with increasing success in the consulting field, you would be remiss not to continually build brands.

## ABANDONING BRANDS

Are there times when brands should be terminated? Or is the hard-won turf of brand uniqueness always worth preserving?

I advise consultants to consider abandoning the bottom 15 percent of their

GM is letting go of Oldsmobile, and Chrysler has abandoned Plymouth. US Airways got rid of "business first." Old brands have to go. It's a pity to see them enfeebled and useless.

I remember watching two kids in a playground while I downed a couple of hot dogs between appointments. When one said that he was stronger (in the game they were fantasizing) because he was "Greatman, saver of the galaxy," his mate reminded him that yesterday he was Aquaman, and needed water to survive.

"That was yesterday," replied Greatman, "and now I've changed who I am."

Even for kids, yesterday's brands just don't cut it.

---

business at least once every two years. That's because you have to let go in order to reach out, and we can't allow precious time, energy, and resources to be usurped by desultory business. In fact, replacing bad business with no business at all—but with the potential to acquire better business—is a quite viable strategy.

The same philosophy can be applied to branding. While you can have an indefinite number of brands, they have to be *the right brands, at the right time, for the right markets.* Therefore, you have to ensure that tired and slumping brands aren't draining your investment that should be placed in dynamic, new branding ventures.

## Checklist: When It's Time to Kiss That Brand Good-Bye

Here are some criteria to use when assessing whether a brand should be abandoned:

- Have new markets been penetrated with the brand? Is it useful in acquiring new buyers, in new demographics, and in desirable new market segments? Does it have appeal to high potential business? *Example:* Does your sales brand transcend from product sales into the newer economies of knowledge and finance?

- Has the brand more potential is its current market, or has it exhausted its potential customer base? *Example:* Does your "Just in Time HR" for the small business market have any more potential customers in New England?
- Is the brand durable and fit for the times, or is it somewhat passé and obsolete? *Example:* Does "Outdoor Experiences" still apply to the current generation of managers, or does it invoke images of Baby Boomers rappelling down mountains?
- Does the brand still have impact? Is it as readily recognizable as it was when created? *Example:* If your name is the brand, but it was based on a book you published fifteen years ago, which is no longer in print, does that name still carry the weight that it once did?

# VIGNETTE

I was called by a management team that requested confidential mentoring, which they paid for out of their own pockets, not the firm's coffers. Their owner and CEO was now in his late fifties and had been the primary rainmaker, based on his very dynamic lecture series in the 1980s and early 1990s. However, he was now wealthy (and the team wasn't), he had severely cut back his public appearances, and he was not nearly as well-known as he had been years ago.

Since the firm's brands all carried his name and references to his speaking aphorisms, their appeal had precipitously dropped, yet the owner was putting pressure on this group to increase profits as he neared his "retirement run." Yet the very fuel for prior profits had been evaporating.

The group had been considering ways in which to get the owner back on the road and in his old form, even though he had shown no inclination or interest to do so. I advised them to abandon that strategy and the old brand, and to create new brands based on the value of the owner's ideas, but not on his name or appearances. The entire operation had a dated image, and they had to shed it overnight and start with a new look.

The jury is still out on their success, but the new approach energized the team and pleased the owner, since his name was still the name of the company.

Relatively few brands last forever, but that's to be expected. After all, it's not the preservation of the brand that is the goal, but the enduring value of the products and services that the brand represents.

- Does the brand anticipate the future? Is it positioned to take advantage of likely new developments in the economy, among buyers, and with new technology? *Example:* "Space age" brands grew into parody when the space age was actually upon us. If the future is about participation and collaboration in the workplace, a brand invoking empowerment would continue to work well, but one connoting independence and individualism might not.
- Does the brand compete aggressively or just barely hold its own? Does it stand out in a crowd? *Example:* If the brand is a sort of middle-of-the-pack hanger-on, you might have accepted mediocrity in your branding efforts. Brands should lead in the niches you have identified. GE insists that its varied divisions be either number one or two in each respective marketplace. It's not unreasonable to abandon brands that aren't, say, in the top ten in your niches.

Abandoning a brand can represent some expense and disruption. But you'll find, if you take an objective and tough view, that such discomfort is well-rewarded in the renewal of your business lines through more contemporary and effective branding efforts.

*Rule of thumb:* Every time you create a new brand, concurrently put all the existing ones through the test above. Even if you don't create new brands, put your current ones to the test every year or so.

## PROTECTING YOUR BRANDS: THE PRINCIPLE OF ADAPTIVE UNIQUENESS

Successful brands become valuable, and protection of brands is an important consideration. However, most people emphasize the wrong kind of protection: legal. More important protection lies in what I call "adaptive uniqueness."

Let's deal with the legalities first. There are copyright, patent, trademark, service mark, and other registration devices available. The ubiquitous ™ symbol is everywhere these days. And it is wise to seek what legal protection you can. This can range from sites on the web, which will do trademark searches for a few hundred dollars and enable you to print out forms to file with the U.S. patent and trademark agencies, to specialized law firms that will conduct extensive research for thousands of dollars.

So, let me say clearly that it's a good idea to seek what legal protection you can. Having said that, let me now say that such protection is hardly air tight and can provide you with a false sense of security. Here's an example.

One of my brands, with my alliance partner, Patricia Fripp, is The Odd Couple™, which is a workshop for speakers on marketing their unique services. Patricia and I are very different types whom no one would expect to find on a stage together (ergo, The Odd Couple, which we originally were considering calling "beauty and the beast," but that's another story). This has become an annual event that draws strong crowds and tremendous business for both of us.

---

The stronger and tighter the law, the more it can be broken or subverted. There is always a chink in the armor or a hole in the wall. But your own uniqueness is not so easily compromised.

---

When we created the concept, we knew we'd need a brand, and joked about The Odd Couple as being perfect, although unfortunately "owned" by Neil Simon or someone associated with the stage and screen hits by that name. When I approached my attorneys with other ideas, I casually mentioned my regrets about what would have been the perfect name, and his reply floored me: "Alan, you may be mistaken; let me look into it for you."

When he saw my shock, he explained (as if to a third-grader, and not a very bright one at that) that trademarks and names can be protected only within the media in which they gained popularity and are used. Because The Odd Couple originally and continually was a stage and screen performance, and Fripp and I were doing educational workshops for speakers, there might well be no conflict.

And, indeed, there wasn't. I had long known that book titles, for example, can't be protected (you can use titles previously used, and it's done all the time, although generally unknown by the public), but this shocked me. In fact, Fripp and I can protect our workshop name against any other workshops on remotely similar topics (but, presumably, we couldn't make a movie about a neatnick and a slob living together).

By all means, consult your own attorney (making sure he or she is expert in this type of law—not all attorneys are, by a long shot) and make your own decisions. But I'm here to tell you that the best legal protection isn't guaranteed to protect your brand or brand name. This is why "Kleenex-brand" tissues, "Formica-brand" countertops, and "Jell-O-brand" gelatin—awkward phrases—have entered the lexicon, since the brand names alone was threatened with becoming generic.

My observation is that you are far safer with so uniquely personalizing your brands that they can't readily be copied, borrowed, subverted, or otherwise appropriated. This personalizing I've come to call "adaptive uniqueness." This is why, although you can use a prior book's title, no one is about to publish a new book called *Gone with the Wind*.

Adaptive uniqueness simply means that you protect your brand(s) by making it so closely associated with you and your work that buyers realize the brand can't be attained without you. If someone wants The Odd Couple experience for marketing speaking skills, they know they must go to Fripp and Weiss. If it's the "Million Dollar Consultant," that's me, because no one else has written *Million Dollar Consulting*. It's not sufficient, however, just to lay claim to the title. I publish continually citing *Million Dollar Consulting*; I use it in headlines and in logos; I speak at seminars and use it in my introduction and handouts. In short, I've established that the brand "Million Dollar Consulting" is synonymous with Alan Weiss, and you can't get the one without the other. The buyer and the public wouldn't settle for someone else using that brand name, even if they had the chutzpah to do so.

So while McDonald's and Disney employ legions of lawyers to sue small shop owners for copyright and brand infringement—usually damaging their own brand and public relations in the process—I'm suggesting that you marry what you do and who you are so closely with your brand that they are inseparable. You need only do this in your primary buying markets, so that is not unduly burdensome, *because these are the markets to which your gravity is addressed in any case.*

> Focus on just one thing in terms of protection if you must: In your primary markets, equate your brand with you, personally, in every way possible, every day. That will be better protection than any firm of legal sharks, no matter how aggressive or hostile.

Adaptive uniqueness is ultimately achieved when your name and image are equated with all of your brands (which is why the ultimate brand is always your name—"Get me Alan Weiss" will only get you Alan Weiss, unless you're in the declining position of "Get me a young Alan Weiss"!). Here are some techniques to ensure adaptive uniqueness:

- Incorporate your brand into your biographical sketch ("the creator of . . ." or "the author of . . ." or "who pioneered. . ."
- Cite your brand in your speeches and conversations with buyers
- Publish extensions of your brand—articles and interviews on how it's used, where it's best employed, how it is evolving, and so on
- Create a logo for the brand that might accompany your own corporate logo at times
- Create a focus on the brand on your website, allied with you and the rest of your work
- Use the brand as an actual title for your talks and articles
- Put the brand on your letterhead and/or business card
- If your name isn't a brand, associate your name with the branded product or service, for example, "John Smith's Teambuilding Cauldron"
- Use the brand as an index for search engines on the web to direct people to you and your site
- Use the brand prominently in your advertising

Protection of your hard-won brands is essential, and legal precautions are prudent and intelligent—and well worth the investment. However, the most effective protection is not in legal documents and filings, but in pragmatic real-world usage. Adaptive uniqueness allows you to meld the brand into your own unique persona, and no one is going to be able to successfully copy that.

*One caveat:* When a brand is successfully and uniquely adapted, it is virtually impossible to transfer to others. Despite noble attempts, branding stars such as Tom Peters, Zig Zigler, Tony Robbins, and others have never been able to establish the networks of trainers for the leverage they sought because people knew the brand was them, not their minions. I think that's a small price to pay, but be aware that you cannot transfer a personalized brand to subordinates, franchisees, or partners. Some of the very best have tried it, and it seldom works. That's how powerful adaptive uniqueness can be.

## KEEPING BRANDS REVITALIZED

Somewhere amidst creating brands, abandoning brands, multiple brands, and other pursuits, you are well-served to continually revitalize and refine the ones that already are working. One reason is that you can almost always do better. And that's not a truism.

The best firms in the world don't spend a lot of time on weaknesses and poor performing areas. Instead, they visit their best operations and decide how to improve them still further. (Hewlett-Packard, for example, is famous for this, continually tearing apart what's already working quite well to try to improve it.) If your brand is working, find out how you can make it even more contemporary, high-impact, and attractive.

> All brands will eventually erode somewhat, and many will atrophy completely, unless carefully tweaked from time to time. Most manufacturers' logos have changed several times, even on highly successful products, and the entire thrust of "reengineering" was its subtitle: reinventing the organization.

The second reason is the "S-Curve" phenomenon, which you'll see in Figure 10.2. Successful brands often create a steep increase in impact (sales, image, repute, word of mouth, etc.). The tendency is to ride the escalator and not worry about it. But all escalators end somewhere, and you have to beware of the plateau, *because all plateaus eventually erode.* So the danger isn't merely in no growth, but in declining growth.

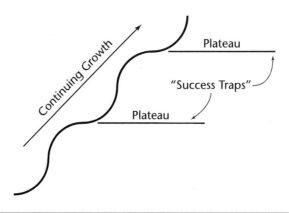

**Figure 10.2.** The Brand Success Trap

Conditions and perceptions change. Sophisticated actors in 1950s films all smoked. Dean Martin once had a popular television show based to no small degree on liquor consumption in huge amounts. Washington named its team "Redskins" before the term was viewed with approbation. Oil crises have come and gone, allies and friends change with amazing rapidity.

Consequently, a brand's rise, no matter what its acceleration and velocity, may end rather abruptly, although at least we notice that "stall." It's far more dangerous and pernicious when the stall is gentle, because we're less apt to note that anything is wrong with the brand. (Disney's brand has undergone subtle changes, for instance, from a family-oriented money machine with gorgeous amusement parks, to a company with adult film subsidiaries, poor earnings, and labor strife.)

The time to make the adjustments and the course corrections is about two-thirds of the way up the slope, not after the plateau hits. (How do you know it's two-thirds of the way?! I'm ahead of you. During times of brand acceleration, examine it for improvement about every six months, regardless of current results.) By "turbocharging" the brand on the ascent, you are able to jump to the next S-curve with maximum thrust and in the shortest relative distance. If you wait for the plateau, you have not only more ground to make up, but virtually no momentum to power the leap.

Here are some areas to examine to renew, revitalize, and refashion even the most successful of brands.

How to Establish a Unique Brand in the Consulting Profession

Not long ago I shared the stage as a keynote speaker with a very well-known sports coach, whose forte is motivation. After my presentation, I remained to watch and learn.

What I saw amazed me. He used locker room examples and jokes, talked about women as if they were all to wait in their nighties (his term) for their men to come home. The room was aghast, since 75 percent of the audience was female.

This was a trip back to the 1950s, and a spiel he's been delivering mindlessly for decades. For him, it's a sideline to his coaching, and he makes a nice buck—even if he's never invited back.

The rest of us can't afford that kind of mental—or brand—obsolescence.

## Ten Techniques to Tweak Brands

1. *Examine the wording, logo, and overall "look" for contemporary society and your most important future markets.* (Even if your name is your brand, is the type font modern, should you add or drop an honorific [Ph.D., MBA], and so on.)
2. *Ask yourself whether it works globally.* Kodak, supposedly, chose that no-meaning assortment of letters because they are, in that sequence, pronounced the same in almost every language in which the company foresaw doing business.
3. *Try to insert it into every aspect of your marketing gravity.* Are there articles, products, speeches, pro bono work, etc., that don't currently convey the brand, but are certainly able to do so.
4. *Explore linkage.* Are you ready to create an umbrella brand to cover all of your products and services, or are you prepared to create additional brands that can fall under an existing umbrella?
5. *Talk to your alliance partners.* Can your brand be inserted—or better inserted—into your mutual working relationship?
6. *Look at the competitive positions.* You shouldn't create brands in response to the competition (but rather in view of your own unique strengths), but you can

examine whether or not your brand is sufficiently taking advantage of the gaps between you and the competition. Try to widen the gaps with more advertising, or larger volume, or further differentiation (for example, "The 21st Century Strategist," and not "Proactive Strategies" or "The Strategist").

7. *Add something to the brand.* Simple words such as "new" and "improved" have always worked in consumer marketing. Consider adding a phrase or word such as "famous" or "unique" or "powerful." There was once a popular speaker whose brand was his name. His name was Charlie Jones, but he billed himself as Charlie Wonderful Jones.

---

Adjustments to a brand may be as simple as changing colors or adding a word. Or they may be as profound as changing the wording or reorienting the emphasis. Try to think of the next market or the next customer, not yesterday's.

---

8. *Look to the future.* Ask yourself who your buyer will be in the next two years and ensure that the brand will appeal to that person. Your current clients and buyers will continue out of loyalty and momentum, so there is little chance of loss and every chance of gain.

9. *Involve your customers and trusted others.* Seek outside commentary on the effectiveness of the brand. Ask some who have no connection with you and no axe to grind or personal agenda. If necessary, commission another consultant to investigate its recognition and impact *while it's effective for you, not after something goes wrong.*

10. *Finally, trust your gut.* Sometimes you'll feel the need for change and renewal yourself. Don't allow a brand, no matter how successful, to manage your practice. *You* have to manage your practice. If you feel that it's time for change, then it probably is. You'll seldom need wholesale change, so simply make the adjustments that give you a new look and a new confidence.

## FINAL THOUGHTS

So, after an entire book on branding for consulting and consultants, where are we? One of the dangers in these intense examinations of specific techniques is that, conceptually, the entire scheme makes sense and, tactically, nothing happens!

I believe in "The 1 Percent Solution™," a realization I had about fifteen years ago. If you improve by 1 percent a day, in seventy days you'll be twice as good as you are today. That's right, just 1 percent a day. The problem, of course, is that most people (and most organizations) don't even manage that modest improvement. Or, worse, they await the epiphany, where everything is supposed to change overnight. But the truth is that we don't normally advance through the invention of fax machines or breakthroughs in new methods to exploit the Internet. We advance by accretion, a little bit at a time, but steadily, every single day. The great organizations are the beneficiaries of tens of thousands of employees trying to work a little smarter and a little better every day, and the poor ones merely house legions of people who can't wait to go home at five.

You probably are your organization, whether or not you have staff or colleagues. Thus, it's up to you to achieve your 1 percent every day. What will it be from this book?

Ideally, you've already adopted some of the principles. (It's not uncommon for people to tell me during my workshops that they used a break or lunchtime to call their office and change an initiative based on what they heard that morning. Presumably, this book took a bit longer to read than that, so you've had time to consider and make some changes.)

## ACTION CHECKLIST

If you haven't yet decided on a course of action, or if you're wondering what additional changes you should make, may I immodestly suggest the following action points for your consideration?

1. Use the "gravity" principle as a starting point. Place the chart on the wall or on your desk, and:

   - Consider any additions to the spokes in the wheel that are feasible for your practice, and write them in
   - Review all the spokes, and make a priority among: those you are doing well, those you are not doing well, and those you are not doing at all

- Ask yourself how you can improve those you already do well (yes, start with your strengths), how you can improve those you don't do well, and which you should begin that you're not doing at all
- Make a basic time line for the improvement actions; plan to have your gravity at least twice as effective in—you guessed it—seventy days

2. Consider your name as a potential brand if it isn't one now, and if it is one, determine how to exploit it still more.

   - Are you attaching your name to a significant number of your marketing plans and delivery activities?
   - If you have current brands, are you associating your name with them (for example, Terri Preston's Team Power Process)?
   - The ultimate brand for the ultimate consultant is your unique name, so focus on how to improve and extend its use

3. Examine the publishing opportunities that exist, in particular, and extend (or initiate) your presence in print.

   - The ultimate printed word for marketing is the book. If you've written one, write another with branding clearly its objective. If you haven't written one, create a "treatment" and pursue an agent or acquisitions editor.
   - Make it a goal to have an article printed every other month somewhere, be it the local newspapers, the Internet, national magazines, or trade association house organs. Create a "body of work."

4. Examine the speaking opportunities that exist, and become comfortable as a spokesperson for your brand.

   - If you need them, take some lessons from a coach or a mentor
   - Use your current clients and contacts to access professional trade associations and management meetings
   - Seek to become a keynote speaker, where your brand and your name will be interrelated in front of thousands of people

5. Re-energize your web presence and print materials. The chances are that they are insufficient in their support of your brands.

- The Internet and your press kit are where many people first "see" you. Ensure that these passive sources are "brand central" and emphasize your main brand, at least.
- Continually test the effectiveness of these materials, and plan to review and improve them at least annually. Structure them so that they are dynamic and easy to change (simple on the web, and also easy in print if you create modular materials).

Plan to do *something* now, and something every week. Managing your brand is like managing your finances. No matter how well you're doing, you need to pay attention. Never be complacent.

The top people in the consulting profession are never content to rest on their laurels or maintain their position. Top people always want to stretch, to improve, and to extend their reach. And top people, presumably, are the ones who are reading these final words.

# Index

Brand success trap, 198*f*

Brand template: four competencies to include in, 16–18; lesson on future use of, 6; themes associated with results for, 23–26. *See also* Consulting brand

Branding: based on repetitive abilities, 24; bell-curve configuration of, 114; "color of the box," 14; copyright/protection of, 194–197; creating vs. default, 4; elitism of, 6, 7, 185–186; importance of "gold standard," 1–2; magnifying, 27–32; negative and positive values of, 3–4; perception of excellence in, 2; real world lessons in, 4–8; value as true secret of, 14–16, 178–180. *See also* Consulting branding

Branding level, 27–28

Branding myths: on brand as external to customer, 123–124; clever catch phrases are sufficient, 114–115; intellectual argument is sufficient, 110–111; on need for specific targets, 116–117; need to analyze environment for need, 112–114; on need for universal recognition, 122–123; regarding advertising, 118; regarding brand value without substance, 125–126; regarding tangible product requirement, 119–120; regarding time of brand development, 115–116; on required brand management, 120–121; restated as positives, 127; on specific/focused nature of brands, 121–122

Branding priorities, 35

Brioni, 179

Bulgari, 179

Burger King, 142, 182

*Business Week*, 52

Business-to-business marketing, 175–176

"Buyer's Guides" listings, 53

## C

Cadillac, 1–2, 185

Calvin Klein, 36, 144

Campbell's Soup, 28

Case Western Reserve, 63

CD-ROM products, 157, 160

*Chemistry Today*, 52

Clancy, T., 126

Client surveys, 23–24

Clients: brand support and needs of, 130; defining your strength through eyes of, 37; increasingly fickle, 182–183; "numero uno" mentality and, 177–178; participation in your branding by, 124; perception of brand name excellence by, 2; referrals, endorsements, testimonials from, 23, 60–61

CMC (Certified Management Consultant), 12

CNN's Gulf War coverage, 116

Co-branding efforts, 35–36

Coca-Cola/Coke, 4–5, 119, 122, 130–131, 143, 182

Commercial publishing activities: boosting your brand through, 154–155; building market gravity through, 45–47

Commercially published book: benefits of, 71–73; choosing a theme for your, 73–74; contingency time frames plan for, 82; creating table of contents for, 74–77; creating/selling proposal for, 77–81; ISBN number of, 161; marketing your, 84–86; process of writing the, 81–84; pros and cons of using an agent, 77–78; reciprocal income created through, 153–154; "reversion of rights" clause in, 87, 155; translated editions of, 154

Competition: benefits of, 142; using brand to advantage in, 199–200

*The Consultant's Craft* (Weiss bi-monthly), 62

*Consultant's News, What's Working in Consulting* (Kennedy Information), 35, 64, 164

Consulting branding: assessing the potential of your, 23–26; ensuring freshness of, 35–36; finding the right recipe for, 22–26; fixing vs. innovating, 188*f*; identifying existing elements of, 21–22; importance of creating, 12, 18; magnifying your, 26–32; payoff of strong, 13–14; professional speaking to promote your, 108; publicizing your, 129–147; re-energizing your, 32–34; strategic branding of, 36–39. *See also* Brand template; Branding

Consulting branding strategies: abandoning brands, 190–193; action checklist for, 201–203; adaptive uniqueness to protect brand, 193–197; final thoughts on, 200–201; keeping brands revitalized, 197–200; multiple brands, 188–190

Consulting branding trends: bang-bang responsiveness, 184; being numero uno, 177–178; briefer attention spans/fickle buyers, 182–183; business-to-business acumen, 175–176; continual enhancement to elite status, 185–186; continuing lack of certification, 173–174; cost-effectiveness/economies of scale, 174–175; differentiation over categorization, 181–182; focus on output, not input, 180–181; increasing stimuli, 170–171; new lessons on, 186; proliferation of products, services, and brands, 172–173; value equation, 178–180

Consulting competencies, 16–18

Consulting products: achieving global appeal through, 154; alliance partners in creating, 35–36, 64–66, 163–164; audio and/or video,

100–101, 156–160; creating reciprocal income through, 153–154; credibility enhanced through, 151; electronic/Internet, 160–163; ethics of producing, 150; ironclad case for, 151–154; new lessons on, 166–167; "no unbundle" policy on, 157; passive income created through, 153; reaching new markets through, 151–152; value to client, 152; Website selling of, 160–162. *See also* Commercially published book

Consulting profession: lack of licensing/certification for, 11, 173–174; need for own brand by, 12, 18; weak associations representing, 11–12

Continental Airlines, 180
Contingency time frames planning, 82
Cooper, W., 164
Corporate branding, 27–28
Credibility: consulting product to enhance, 151; establishing, 171; teaching to enhance, 63–64
Cross pens, 141
CVS drug store change, 35

**D**

Daimler-Benz, 149
Datsun, 150
Delta Airlines, 130
*The Directory of Memberships and News Sources*, 49
Disney, 6, 195, 198
Disney, W., 6
Drucker, P., 34, 84, 121
"Duck Tape" brand name, 31

**E**

Edsel, 121, 144
Electronic newsletters, 56–58, 162
Electronic/internet products, 160–163
Elitism: branding, 6; continual enhancement of brand, 185–186; of Mercedes brand name, 1, 2, 185; perception of, 7
Email signature file, 138, 162
Endorsements, 23, 60–61
Erhard Seminar Training (est), 34n.8, 123
Erhard, W., 34n.8, 123

**F**

FedEx, 9, 13, 27n.4, 31, 114, 140, 182
Ferrari, 36, 107, 141, 179, 185
Fleet Bank, 28
Ford, 119
Formica, 31, 140, 141
Forrest, N. B., 140
*Fortune* magazine, 2

Friedman, N., 8, 30, 141, 176n.1
Fripp, P., 129, 194, 195

**G**

GE (General Electric), 119, 193
Gillette, 107, 121
Gillette, K., 121
GM (General Motors), 34, 191
"Gold standard" brand, 1–2
Gore, A., 170
Gravity principle. *See* Marketing gravity
Greyhound, 182
*The Guide to Periodic Literature*, 46n.3

**H**

Hammer, M., 121, 146
Handouts/visual aids, 96–97, 98
*Harvard Business Review*, 52
Herman, J., 81n.2
Hertz, 177
Hewlett-Packard, 121, 151, 171, 197
High priced brand, 165
"Hollywood phenomenon," 32
*How to Establish Value-Based Fees* (Weiss), 164n.4
*How to Market, Establish a Brand, and Sell Services* (Weiss), 164n.4
*How to Maximize Fees in Professional Service Firms* (Weiss), 155
*How to Write a Proposal That's Accepted Every Time* (Weiss), 23n.2, 164n.4
*HRMagazine*, 52

**I**

IBM, 3, 13, 119, 120, 121, 140, 171, 176
IMC (Institute of Management Consultants), 11, 60, 174
Infiniti automobile, 114
Information overload, 170
*The Innovation Formula* (Weiss and Robert), 76
Institute of Management Studies, 63
*Insurance News*, 52
Intel, 121
Internet: business-to-business marketing of, 175–176; online presentations via the, 163n.3; products through the, 160–163. *See also* Websites
Interviews, 23, 48–51, 63
ISBN number, 161
Ivory Soap, 115

**J**

Jaguar, 5–6
Jobs, S., 120
Johnny Walker, 190

Johnson, S., 146
Jones, C., 200

## K

Kennedy Information, 35, 36, 64–65, 119, 144, 163, 164
Kepner, C., 139
Kepner-Tregoe, 139, 142
KFC (Kentucky Fried Chicken), 145
Kleenex, 31, 119, 141, 176
Kodak, 14, 111, 140, 180
"Kodak moments," 140

## L

Lardo, V., 126
*The Learning Organization*, 67
Lecture circuit: estimate and range of U.S., 90–91; public speaking vs. professional, 89–90. *See also* Professional speaking
Lexus, 28n.5, 142, 145
Linked brands, 189–190, 199
Logos, 144, 146, 185, 199

## M

McDonald's, 122, 130, 142, 143, 145, 182, 195
McKinsey, 3, 27, 31, 132, 140, 177
"McNally" book series, 125–126
Mapes, H., 60
Marketing gravity: advertising as, 51–52; alliances to generate, 64–66; assessing your, 23–24; communicating your brands as part of, 38–39; electronic newsletters to generate, 56–58; elements of, 41–43, 42f; keeping your name aligned with, 32; to maneuver in modern market, 175; networking to generate, 67–69; passive listings to generate, 52–53; position papers to generate, 47–48; print newsletters to generate, 61–63; pro bono work to generate, 44–45; products to generate, 66–67; radio, television, and print interviews for, 23, 48–51, 63; speaking to generate, 54–55; teaching credibility to generate, 63–64; third-party referrals, endorsements, testimonials for, 23, 60–61; trade association leadership to generate, 59–60; websites used to generate, 55–56; word of mouth to generate, 58–59. *See also* Commercially published book; Publishing activities
Marketing your book, 84–86
Marriott, 144
Mars Company, 30
Marshall, P., 126
Martin, D., 198
Maybach, 130
Maytag repairman brand, 7

MCI, 117
Media appearances, 23, 48–51
Mercedes: creation of brand name of, 149–150; high quality/elitism brand name of, 1, 2, 185; lower price/high quality strata strategy by, 130, 144, 190; unifying branding used by, 28; value implied by branding of, 15, 16, 119
"Mercedes-Benz syndrome," 105–106
Merck & Co., 108, 149, 150
Merrill Lynch, 31
Merrill, R., 34
Microsoft, 13, 176
Miller Beer/Miller Time, 5, 34, 115
*Million Dollar Consulting* (Weiss), 47, 195
Ming the Merciless, 43
MiracleGro brand, 7–8
Miss Piggy brand, 6–7
*Money Talks: How to Make a Million As a Speaker* (Weiss), 54n.6
*Money Talks*, 54n.7
Montblanc pens, 141, 185
Morita, A., 112, 114
Multiple brands: using independent, 188–189; using linked, 189–190

## N

NameSecure.com, 32n.7
National Speakers Association, 173
Negative brand, 3–4, 5–6, 116
Networking, 67–69
"New Coke" fiasco, 4–5, 130–131
New England Speakers Association, 59
*New York Times*, 170
Newsletter: electronic, 162; print, 61–63, 162
Niche brands, 8, 35, 177
Nissan, 150
Northern California Chapter (IMC), 60
"Numero uno" mentality, 177–178

## O

The Odd Couple (Weiss-Fripp workshop), 194, 195
*The One Minute Manager* (Blanchard), 67, 153
The 1 Percent Solution, 201
Online presentations, 163n.3
*Our Emperors Have No Clothes* (Weiss), 152

## P

Palm Pilot, 115
Pan Am, 185
Passive income, 153
Passive listings, 52–53
Perception: of brand name excellence, 2; as reality, 3–4, 51

Personal name branding, 31–32, 196
Peters, T., 121, 146, 197
Pinto, 144
*Playboy* magazine, 121
Poland Spring, 33
Position paper, 47–48
Press kits, 102, 138, 155
Principle of adaptive uniqueness, 193–197
Print consulting products, 61–63, 154–155, 162.
     *See also* Commercially published book
Print interviews, 23, 48–51, 63
Print newsletters, 61–63, 162
"Private label" mentality, 353
Pro bono work, 44–45
Procter & Gamble, 28n.5, 144, 188
Products: alliances for, 163–166; branding myth
     regarding tangible, 119–120; creation of,
     66–67; ethics of consultant producing, 150;
     ironclad case for consulting profession,
     151–154
Professional speaking: charges/rights to record,
     159n.2; creating simple architecture for, 93;
     elements of powerful delivery of, 97–100;
     exploiting success in, 106–108; insider tips on,
     91–97; opportunities for, 90–91; promoting
     brand awareness through, 108; public speak-
     ing vs., 89–90; setting fees for, 104–106; 3R
     formula for questions, 99–100; turbo-market-
     ing your, 100–104. *See also* Lecture circuit
Professional speaking marketing: audio and/or
     video presentation for, 100–101; checklist for,
     100–101; press kit adapted for, 102; using
     speakers bureaus for, 102–104, 159; testimoni-
     als used for, 101–102
Professional speaking tips: Alan's quick speech
     methods for, 92–93; choosing theme tied to
     brand, 93; creating powerful five-minute clos-
     ing, 96; creating visual aids/handouts, 96–97,
     98; organize content around 45 minute seg-
     ment, 95–96; orient speech around benefits to
     listener, 93–94; using powerful two-minute
     opening, 94; preparation from audience's per-
     spective, 91–93
*Providence Business News,* 47
Publicizing brand: importance of, 129–130; new
     lessons for, 147; twenty-five ideas for foster-
     ing, 139–147. *See also* Brand environment
Publishing activities: commercial, 45–47,
     154–155; self-publishing vs. commercial,
     45n.2, 72, 87n.4; themes used in your, 23. *See
     also* Commercially published book

**R**
Radio interviews, 23, 48–51, 63
*Radio and TV Interview Reporter,* 49

The Rainmaker series, 164
"Rainmaking: Strategies for Consulting Suc-
     cess" (Weiss seminar series), 36
RC cola, 182
Re-energizing brand: appropriate situations for,
     33–34; avoiding brand plateaus, 33*f*
Referrals, 23
"Response statement," 45
Responsiveness brand, 184
"Reversion of rights" clause, 87, 155
Revitalizing brands, 197–200
RFPs (Request for Proposals), 66, 72
Ritz-Carlton, 144
Robbins, T., 197
Robert, M., 76
Rolex, 141, 179
Rolls-Royce, 130
Rolodex, 140

**S**
S-Curve phenomenon, 197–198*f*
Sali, S., 186
Sanders, L., 125, 126
Self-publishing, 45n.2, 72, 87n.4
Service group branding, 29
7UP, 131
Simon, N., 194
Sinatra, F., 125
"The Small Business MBA" (Weiss weekly col-
     umn), 47
Sony, 112
Southwest Airlines, 6, 115, 145
Speakers bureaus, 102–104, 159
Speaking engagements, 54–55. *See also* Profes-
     sional speaking
Speech themes, 23
Sprint, 117
"Stories I Could Never Tell" (Weiss video), 160
Strategic branding, 36–39, 38*f*
Summit Consulting Group, 178

**T**
Teaching credibility, 63–64
"The Team Builder" (Weiss), 49
The Telephone Doctor, 8, 30, 141, 176
Television interviews, 23, 48–51, 63
Testimonials: client, 23, 60–61; speaking effec-
     tiveness, 101–102
"Thinking from the outside in" process, 130
Third-party referrals, 23, 60–61
3R formula for questions, 99–100
Tide, 115, 119
Times Mirror Group, 151
Timex, 141
TMTE (to maximize the effectiveness): of

advertising, 52; of alliance partners, 66; of commercial publishing, 47; of electronic newsletters, 57–58; of media appearances/ interviews, 50–51; of networking, 69; of position papers, 48; of print newsletters, 62–63; of pro bono work, 44–45; of product creation, 67; of speaking engagements, 55; of teaching credibility, 64; of testimonials, 61; of trade association leadership, 60; of word of mouth, 59

Towers Perrin, 28

Toyota, 28n.5, 142, 145

Trade association leadership, 59–60

*Training & Development,* 52

*Training Magazine,* 52

Tregoe, B., 139

Tylenol, 107

## U

Ultimate marketeer checklist, 84–86

Umbrella brand, 189–190, 199

Unifying branding, 28–29

United Airlines, 180

Universal recognition, 122–123

US Airways, 130, 181, 191

U.S. Marines brand, 7

## V

Value: to the customer, 15*f;* defining your consulting, 143; importance of having brand, 125–126; negative vs. positive branding, 3–4; as ultimate secret of branding, 14–16, 178–180

Value equation, 178–180

Video and/or audio marketing tools, 100–101, 156–160

Virgin Airlines, 115

"Virtual consulting team" experience, 25

Visual aids/handouts, 96–97, 98

## W

*Wall Street Journal,* 117

Websites: arranging for registration of, 32n.7; assessing interest aspects of your, 23; as "brand central" location, 138; making products available on your, 160–162; marketing gravity generated using, 55–56; marketing gravity rules on, 42; modern appeal of using, 146; personal name, 32; publishers' guidelines found on, 81n.2; speaking activities addressed on your, 102. *See also* Internet

Weiss, A., 31, 32, 36, 38–39, 58, 61, 124, 176, 195, 196

*What's Working in Consulting* (Weiss monthly), 62, 164n.5

"White paper," 47–48

Word of mouth, 58–59

Writer's block formula, 82–83

*Writer's Digest,* 46n.3

*Writer's Market,* 46n.3

## X

Xerox, 31

## Y

Yahoo, 115

*The Yearbook of Experts, Authorities & Spokespersons,* 48–49

Yellow Pages listings, 53

## Z

Zigler, Z., 197